The "I Love Lucy" Book of Trivia

Ric B. Wyman

FRIEDMAN/FAIRFAX

ACKNOWLEDGMENTS

A million thanks to the following friends, whose encouragement, help, and support made *The "I Love Lucy" Book of Trivia* a reality: Nate Arnone, Lorra-Lea Bartlett, Kathleen Brady, Pat Brininger, Bruce Bronn, Madelyn Pugh Davis, Nan Eaker, Elisabeth Edwards (you deserve a loving cup!), Brian Eich, Marty Garcia, Patti Pesavento, John Schillner, Melody Thomas Scott, Wanda Clark Stamatovich, Brandon Swarthout, Keith Thibodeaux, Norman Van Vlack, and Kathy Wittman. Special thanks to Lucie Arnaz for her ongoing support.

Many thanks to Sharyn Rosart, who believed in this work and entrusted it to the very capable hands of my editor, Nathaniel Marunas. Thank you, Nathaniel, for guiding me through the unique demands of writing a trivia book and for successfully balancing persistence with patience.

Finally, I express my sincere gratitude to Desi Arnaz, Jr. for agreeing to participate in the creation of this book and for the confidence in the work his gesture conveys.

In memory of *"I Love Lucy"*'s Mr. Littlefield, Gale Gordon, and Lucille's lifelong friend, Marion Strong Van Vlack

A FRIEDMAN/FAIRFAX BOOK
© 2001 by Michael Friedman Publishing Group, Inc.
Text © 2001 Ric Wyman

Please visit our website: www.metrobooks.com

Grateful acknowledgment is given to the writers of *"I Love Lucy"* whose work is quoted in this book:
Jess Oppenheimer, Madelyn Pugh Davis, Bob Carroll, Jr., Bob Schiller, and Bob Weiskopf.

Library of Congress Cataloging-in-Publication Data available upon request.

ISBN 1-58663-145-4

Editors: Nathaniel Marunas and Sharyn Rosart
Art Director: Jeff Batzli
Designer: Lynne Yeamans
Cover Design: Kevin Baier
Photography Editor: Chris Bain
Production Manager: Richela Fabian Morgan

Color separations by Radstock Reproductions Ltd.
Printed in England by Butler & Tanner Ltd.

1 3 5 7 9 10 8 6 4 2

Distributed by Sterling Publishing Company, Inc.
387 Park Avenue South
New York, NY 10016
Distributed in Canada by Sterling Publishing
Canadian Manda Group
One Atlantic Avenue, Suite 105
Toronto, Ontario, Canada M6K 3E7
Distributed in Australia by
Capricorn Link (Australia) Pty. Ltd.
P.O. Box 704, Windsor, NSW 2756 Australia

About this Book

For fifty years, the groundbreaking, now-classic television show *"I Love Lucy"* has been welcomed into millions of homes throughout the world. Today, the antics of the Ricardos and Mertzes remain a daily part of millions of people's lives—not only in the United States and Canada, but also in Brazil, Bolivia, Ecuador, Greece, Hong Kong, Italy, Spain, Singapore, and more than thirty other countries around the globe.

The *"I Love Lucy" Book of Trivia* celebrates the magic of *"I Love Lucy"* and its over-whelming appeal with a collection of thousands of trivia questions about Lucy, Ricky, Fred, and Ethel, whose escapades continue to bring laughter to the show's devoted fans. The classic episodes bear watching again and again—and there are plenty of fans, maybe you included, who know each one intimately. Or do you? This book will reveal just how much you have really absorbed.

If you know Lucy Ricardo's dress size, here's your chance to prove it! Maybe you can recite the classic "Vitameatavegamin" commercial speech. Perhaps you'd like to show how much you know about Ricky Ricardo's family history (it's "relatively" easy—see quiz #52), and if you're a fan of Mrs. Mertz, then puzzle #8, "Everything Ethel," is for you. There's even a quiz devoted exclusively to chickens...and it's all done in the name of Lucy.

The *"I Love Lucy" Book of Trivia* also serves as a reference, featuring a listing of each and every *"I Love Lucy"* episode title and original broadcast date. You'll find this episode log, which begins on page 126, handy when a trivia question has you stumped. When you check your answers in the answer key, you'll usually find a number in parentheses that refers to the episode in which the correct answer can be found. When there is no number in parentheses after the answer, the question pertains to more than one episode or to the show as a whole. And if you're completely unable to answer a question—even with help from the episode log—check the answer key, which begins on page 132.

Okay. Now you know all about this book...but what do you know about *"I Love Lucy"*? It's time to turn the page and join the "thousands of happy, peppy people" in a journey into loving cups, bonus bucks, and laughter with The *"I Love Lucy" Book of Trivia*.

—Ric Wyman, Director
The Lucy-Desi Museum
Jamestown, New York

Foreword

Mom and Dad would have been as surprised as anyone to learn that, after fifty years, *"I Love Lucy"* is still one of the most watched and loved shows on television. I also think they would have been extraordinarily pleased that *"I Love Lucy"* is still shown all over the world.

The *"I Love Lucy"* show is still on the air because it hits you on a lot of different levels. A story about an American woman married to a Cuban bandleader was unprecedented then and remains unique today. It wasn't the everyday story people were used to seeing in films or on television.

Mom and Dad had to work hard to convince CBS and their sponsors that the show was something that television viewers would want to see. No one would even listen to them until they had taken an early version of the show on the road as a vaudeville act for six months. The overwhelming response they got on that tour helped persuade the network to give them a try. And even then they had to come up with the funding for a pilot on their own. Maybe that's why they loved *"I Love Lucy"* so much: they truly put so much of themselves into it.

The interracial marriage component was just one of the groundbreaking aspects of the show. They also came up with new ways of filming a television show in front of a live audience, including flat lighting, innovative camera and dolly work, and much more. And recording *"I Love Lucy"* on film may have been the most profound new direction they took. This allowed them to work in California and still present an "original" show to New York audiences, all the while preserving a kind of ongoing home movie for Lucie and me. Mom and Dad would never have guessed that the show would pretty much invent the syndicated rerun—and that one day *"I Love Lucy"* could be seen (according to *TV Guide*) 24 hours a day, 7 days a week, somewhere in the world (in 77 different countries, in 22 languages!).

Another groundbreaker was Mom's appearing on television when she was expecting me. When her pregnancy threatened to end the show, Dad and his creative partners found a way to make the most popular show on television even more popular. And although the word "pregnant" could never be uttered on the air, the viewing public were so enthralled with the event that 44 million of them watched Little Ricky's birth on the day I was born, January 19, 1953.

It's very powerful for me to watch the show because of the pregnancy and things that were going on in real life. Dad wrote "There's a Brand New Baby at Our House" for my sister, but then sang it on the show for Little Ricky. He then sang another song, "We're Having a Baby," for me. It's not just funny, it's also heartwarming—there's rarely a dry eye when viewers watch Lucy telling Ricky "the news."

Even knowing how many people around the planet love the show, the number of fans who know the smallest details about the most popular show on television is truly amazing. My thanks to Ric Wyman for giving *"I Love Lucy"* fans this wonderful opportunity to test their skills, learn even more about the show, and laugh again at Mom and Dad's wonderful creation!

—Desi Arnaz, Jr.

1 First Things First

Here are ten questions devoted to some *"I Love Lucy"* firsts.

1 Who is the first star Lucy spots in Hollywood?

  A Cary Grant

  B William Holden

  C Eve Arden

  D none of these

2 What is the title of the first episode that includes Keith Thibodeaux as Little Ricky?

3 True or false: Mrs. Trumbull first appeared in episode 26, "The Marriage License."

4 Who is the first person to suspect that Lucy is going to have a baby?

  A Lucy's doctor

  B Lucy

  C Mrs. Trumbull

  D Ethel

5 Mr. Chambers, Ricky's nightclub boss, is first mentioned in:

  A "Ricky Asks for a Raise"

  B "Ricky Loses His Voice"

  C "Ricky Has Labor Pains"

  D "The French Revue"

6 In "The Indian Show," what does Little Ricky do for the very first time?

7 Name the episode that includes the word "first" in the title.

8 Choose the episode that wasn't part of *"I Love Lucy"*'s first season of shows:

  A "Lucy Writes a Play"

  B "Lucy Does a TV Commercial"

  C "Job Switching"

  D "The Ballet"

9 In "The Quiz Show," Lucy appears on the radio show *Females Are Fabulous*. What does Lucy have to do to win the thousand-dollar jackpot?

10 Tennessee Ernie Ford appeared in three *"I Love Lucy"* episodes. Can you name the episode title and number of the first of these three classic shows?

Seein' Stars

Name the celebrity Lucy Ricardo is impersonating in each picture below.

3 All About Lucy

Prove yourself a true fan of the wacky redhead by answering all twenty of these Lucy Ricardo trivia questions without hesitation.

1. What year was Lucy Ricardo born?
2. What is Lucy's middle name?
3. Name the publishing house that paid Lucy an advance on her book.
4. What was Lucy's grade school nickname?
5. In "The Quiz Show," what is Lucy's system for paying bills?
6. What is Lucy's dress size?
7. What is Lucy's true hair color?
8. What is Lucy's favorite breakfast?
9. As a playwright, Lucy pens a "tender, heartwarming story about a Cuban tobacco picker." Name the play.
10. What three-letter word lands Lucy in a Tennessee jail?
11. What inspires Lucy to become an author in "Lucy Writes a Novel"?
12. Name Lucy's hairdresser, as mentioned in "The Black Wig."
13. In "Lucy's Show Biz Swan Song," who does Lucy replace as the fourth member of the barbershop quartet?
14. When is Lucy's birthday?
15. In episode 72 we learn Lucy's weight. How much does she weigh?
16. With Ethel as her partner, Lucy goes into the fashion business. From whom do the women buy a dress shop?
17. Name the famous Native American Lucy once portrayed in a school pageant.
18. What was Lucy's "million-dollar idea"?
19. To which women's club does Lucy Ricardo belong?
20. What is Lucy's maiden name?

AKA Lucy

Lucy Ricardo was a lady of a thousand laughs—and a thousand different looks. Identify the character Lucy is portraying in each of these photographs from some of Mrs. Ricardo's most unforgettable misadventures.

A _____

B _____

C _____

D _____

E _____

F _____

G _____

H _____

I _____

5 Remembering Ricky

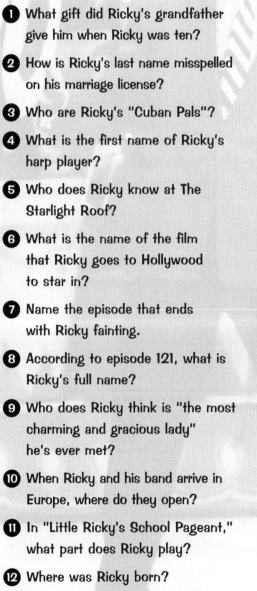

1. What gift did Ricky's grandfather give him when Ricky was ten?

2. How is Ricky's last name misspelled on his marriage license?

3. Who are Ricky's "Cuban Pals"?

4. What is the first name of Ricky's harp player?

5. Who does Ricky know at The Starlight Roof?

6. What is the name of the film that Ricky goes to Hollywood to star in?

7. Name the episode that ends with Ricky fainting.

8. According to episode 121, what is Ricky's full name?

9. Who does Ricky think is "the most charming and gracious lady" he's ever met?

10. When Ricky and his band arrive in Europe, where do they open?

11. In "Little Ricky's School Pageant," what part does Ricky play?

12. Where was Ricky born?

13. Who is Ricky's barber?

14. Name all five of Ricky's brothers.

15. What gift did Ricky's band give him for Christmas in 1952?

16. What is the name of Ricky's nightclub?

17. What was Ricky's role in Lucy's operetta?

18. Before landing a job at the Copacabana, where did Ricky appear?

19. With which professional golfer did Ricky once play?

20. What is the first name of Ricky's pianist?

21. Ricky loves chicken and rice. What is his other favorite food?

22. According to Lucy, how tall is Ricky?

23. According to Ricky, what word is the same in English, Spanish, and French?

24. As mentioned in "Home Movies," who, according to Ricky, is the most important man in television?

Occupational Hazard

Complete the crossword puzzle below by identifying the character or the occupation for each clue provided.

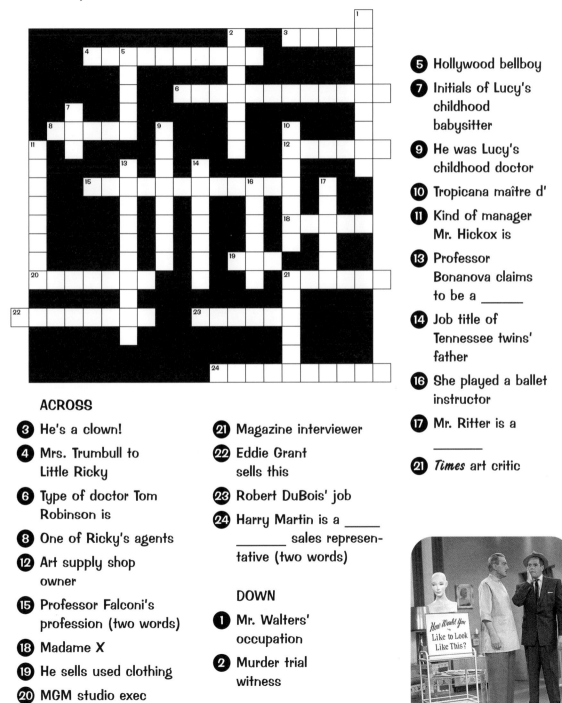

5 Hollywood bellboy

7 Initials of Lucy's childhood babysitter

9 He was Lucy's childhood doctor

10 Tropicana maître d'

11 Kind of manager Mr. Hickox is

13 Professor Bonanova claims to be a _____

14 Job title of Tennessee twins' father

16 She played a ballet instructor

17 Mr. Ritter is a _____

21 *Times* art critic

ACROSS

3 He's a clown!

4 Mrs. Trumbull to Little Ricky

6 Type of doctor Tom Robinson is

8 One of Ricky's agents

12 Art supply shop owner

15 Professor Falconi's profession (two words)

18 Madame X

19 He sells used clothing

20 MGM studio exec

21 Magazine interviewer

22 Eddie Grant sells this

23 Robert DuBois' job

24 Harry Martin is a _____ _____ sales representative (two words)

DOWN

1 Mr. Walters' occupation

2 Murder trial witness

Friends and Neighbors I

Can you identify these *"I Love Lucy"* friends and neighbors?

A _____ D _____ G _____

B _____ E _____ H _____

C _____ F _____ I _____

Everything Ethel

Here's a multiple-choice quiz devoted to the lady Fred calls "honeybunch."

1 Ethel's wedding anniversary is:
- **A** March 11
- **B** April 1
- **C** May 3
- **D** June 11

2 Which of Ethel's old boyfriends is a newspaper reporter?
- **A** Billy Hackett
- **B** Hank Spear
- **C** Deak Arley
- **D** none of these

3 Ethel's father's name is:
- **A** Will
- **B** Bill
- **C** Hank
- **D** Ben

4 Why was Ethel once in Minnesota?
- **A** She attended a family reunion held in Minnesota.
- **B** She was born in Minnesota.
- **C** She went to Minnesota for surgery.
- **D** She attended a Minnesota school.

5 Ethel Mertz did not appear in which of these *I Love Lucy* episodes?
- **A** "The Quiz Show"
- **B** "The Benefit"
- **C** "Cuban Pals"
- **D** "Lucy Does a TV Commercial"

6 In which episode does Ethel refer to Lucy as "Sleepytime Gal"?
- **A** "Home Movies"
- **B** "Bonus Bucks"
- **C** "Lucy Writes a Novel"
- **D** "Lucy's Club Dance"

7 What is Ethel's astrological sign?
- **A** Leo
- **B** Libra
- **C** Scorpio
- **D** Taurus

8 Ethel claims to be a home economist on which program?
- **A** *Good Morning, New York*
- **B** *The Freddy Fillmore Show*
- **C** *The Dickie Davis Show*
- **D** *Females are Fabulous*

9 Ethel's Aunt Emmy is married to a retired butcher. What's his name?
- **A** Bud
- **B** Oscar
- **C** Mayer
- **D** Frank

10 Ethel played _____ in "The Operetta."
- **A** Millie
- **B** Tillie
- **C** Lily
- **D** Blanche

11 Ethel's hometown newspaper is:

A *The Daily Herald*

B *The Tribune*

C *The Chronicle*

D *The Press Gazette*

12 Ethel's Uncle Elmo is married to:

A Aunt Martha   **C** Aunt Irene

B Aunt Esther   **D** Aunt Mary

13 Who said, "Ethel has the habit of staying on a subject until it gets sickening"?

A Lucy   **C** Fred

B Ricky   **D** Betty

14 Ethel studied _____ in high school.

A French   **C** German

B Spanish   **D** Italian

15 Ethel Mertz does not appear in which *"I Love Lucy"* episode?

A "The Moustache"

B "The Young Fans"

C "The Publicity Agent"

D "The Courtroom"

16 What kind of business does Ethel's father run?

A ice cream shop

B drugstore

C sweet shop and soda fountain

D newspaper

17 Which of the following is *not* one of Ethel's middle names?

A Lou   **C** Roberta

B Mae   **D** Louise

18 When packing for their European trip, whose luggage does Ethel borrow?

A Mrs. Trumbull's

B Mrs. McGillicuddy's

C Martha's

D Carolyn's

19 Ethel once worked at a diner in which Midwestern city?

A Toledo

B Steubenville

C Indianapolis

D Detroit

Going Places 9

Complete the titles of the *"I Love Lucy"* episodes listed below by inserting names of places that the Ricardos and Mertzes have traveled to.

1 "Visitor from _____ "

2 " _____ Bound"

3 " _____ , Here We Come"

4 "In _____ _____ " (2 words)

5 " _____ Anniversary"

6 "Lucy Goes to _____ "

7 "Lucy Goes to _____ _____ " (2 words)

8 "Lucy in the _____ _____ " (2 words)

9 "Ricky's _____ Vacation"

10 "Off to _____ "

11 " _____ _____ Ferry" (2 words)

12 " _____ at Last"

13 "Return Home from _____ "

14 "Ricardos Visit _____ "

10 Brown Derby Dining

Lucy and the Mertzes visit The Brown Derby with hopes of seeing some "real live movie stars" in episode 114, "L.A. at Last." In this famous episode, Lucy ends up causing a tray of desserts to spill on William Holden. But before Holden gets covered in whipped cream, Lucy, Ethel, and Fred are able to order from the menu, spot a few celebrities, and enjoy the famous Hollywood eatery.

1 Choosing the best answer for each, match the entree with the person who ordered it:

Lucy

Ethel

Fred

William Holden

A Cobb Salad and a cup of coffee

B Spaghetti

C Derby Toss Salad

D Derby Toss Salad and spaghetti and meatballs with lots of meat sauce

E Veal Cutlet Marco Polo

F Cobb Salad

2 While Lucy and the Mertzes are dining at the Derby, three movie stars are paged for phone calls. Who are they?

3 Name the waiter who serves both Lucy and William Holden.

4 Who spots William Holden first?

A Lucy

B Ethel

C Fred

D Lucy, Ethel, and Fred see Holden walk in at the same time

5 What does Ethel pull out of her purse to aid Lucy in eating her lunch?

6 True or false: The Brown Derby Restaurant can be seen from the balcony of the Ricardos' hotel suite?

7 What celebrity's caricature takes up two frames on the wall over the booth where Lucy, Ethel, and Fred are sitting?

Hollywood Souvenirs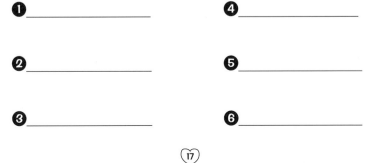

In addition to Lana Turner's lipstick print, can you identify the other souvenirs Lucy collected while in Hollywood? Need help? Just watch episode 128, "Lucy Visits Grauman's."

① _____   ④ _____

② _____   ⑤ _____

③ _____   ⑥ _____

12: The Candy Factory

We all remember Lucy and Ethel's unsuccessful attempt at wrapping chocolates at a candy factory, but can you recall the answers to the following trivia questions without watching this classic episode for clues?

1 Why is Ethel's checking account never overdrawn?

2 What is the name of the employment agency that places Lucy and Ethel?

3 What is the motto of this employment agency?

4 Before being considered for the candy maker jobs, Lucy and Ethel are considered for six other occupations. Name them.

5 Name the candy company that hires Lucy and Ethel.

6 Why does Lucy slap her candy-dipping coworker in the face?

7 Why was Ethel removed from the boxing department?

8 In addition to the boxing department, how many other departments was Ethel given a chance in before being transferred to the wrapping department?

9 Swapping places with their wives, Ricky and Fred stay at home and soon discover for themselves that housework isn't easy. What two household chores do they fail at?

10 What does Ricky use to clean the chicken he's preparing for dinner?

11 Fred and Ricky cook dinner together—Ricky decides to cook the main course, Fred, the dessert. What does Fred attempt to make?

12 After realizing how tough it is to run a house, Ricky and Fred go out to buy gifts for their wives. What gifts make Lucy and Ethel cringe?

13 Before getting fired, what is the last department Lucy and Ethel work in?

14 How does Ricky trick Lucy into thinking he's a good cook?

15 Ricky asks Fred what he knows about rice. What is Fred's answer?

16 According to the sign hanging inside the agency office, who is the president of the employment agency?

17 How much rice does Ricky prepare for dinner?

18 Lucy wrote a note on the back of a rubber check. What does the note say?

19 To whom did Lucy issue the check?
   A the butcher
   B Hansen's Dress Shop
   C the beauty parlor
   D herself

20 In this episode, the Ricardos receive one phone call. Who called and why?

13 That's English?

Throughout the years on *I Love Lucy*, Lucy playfully teases Ricky about his Cuban accent. See if you can match what Ricky was heard saying on the show (in column A) to what he meant to say (in column B).

COLUMN A	COLUMN B
1 dip-see	psychiatrist
2 "spin the beans out of the cat bag"	"you have made your bed, now lie in it"
3 ma-gill-a-cooty	"spill the beans" and "let the cat out of the bag"
4 strav-a-gan-zas	gossiping
5 fizz-ee-a-key-a-trist	"the die is cast"
6 "yelling tiger"	extravagances
7 gos-pen	jealous
8 interior motive	ulterior motive
9 "stew in her own goose"	deep sea
10 "jumped her trolley"	"her goose is cooked" and "stew in her own juices"
11 yell-us	don't
12 spear-ee-ins	"off her trolley"
13 "the cast is dead"	McGillicuddy
14 dunt	experience
15 "you have fixed the sheets and blankets, now go take a nap"	"crying wolf"

My Favorite Redhead  14

Which of these *"I Love Lucy"* episodes were based on episodes from Lucy's earlier CBS radio series, *My Favorite Husband* (1948–51)?

1. "The Seance"
2. "Lucy's Last Birthday"
3. "Lucy Is Matchmaker"
4. "Changing the Boys' Wardrobe"
5. "Lucy Changes Her Mind"
6. "Lucy Becomes a Sculptress"
7. "The Marriage License"
8. "The Gossip"
9. "Men Are Messy"
10. "Country Club Dance"
11. "Be a Pal"
12. "The Girls Go into Business"

13. "The Inferiority Complex"
14. "The Passports"
15. "Ricky Asks for a Raise"
16. "The Quiz Show"
17. "Lucy Learns to Drive"
18. "The Black Eye"
19. "Vacation from Marriage"
20. "The Club Election"
21. "The Diet"
22. "Lucy's Schedule"
23. "Lucy Tells the Truth"
24. "The French Revue"
25. "The Handcuffs"

1. There are ___ episodes of *"I Love Lucy"* in syndication.
   - Ⓐ 144
   - Ⓑ 156
   - Ⓒ 179
   - Ⓓ 181

2. During which season do the Ricardos and Mertzes travel to California?
   - Ⓐ 1952–53 (second season)
   - Ⓑ 1953–54 (third season)
   - Ⓒ 1954–55 (fourth season)
   - Ⓓ 1955–56 (fifth season)

3. *"I Love Lucy"* was usually filmed on one of two days a week. What were the two days?

4. True or false: Studio audience members under the age of 16 were not admitted.

5. Name the two writers who were credited in every *"I Love Lucy"* episode.

6. *"I Love Lucy"* was originally telecast on the _____ network.
   - Ⓐ ABC
   - Ⓑ CBS
   - Ⓒ DuPont
   - Ⓓ NBC

7. The original sponsor for the series was:
   - Ⓐ Jello
   - Ⓑ Chesterfield
   - Ⓒ Philip Morris
   - Ⓓ Ford Motor Company

8. Name the three original writers of *"I Love Lucy."*

9. *"I Love Lucy"* debuted on a _____ night.
   - Ⓐ Sunday
   - Ⓑ Monday
   - Ⓒ Tuesday
   - Ⓓ Thursday

10. What is the exact date *"I Love Lucy"* was seen on television for the very first time?

Food for Thought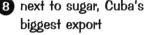

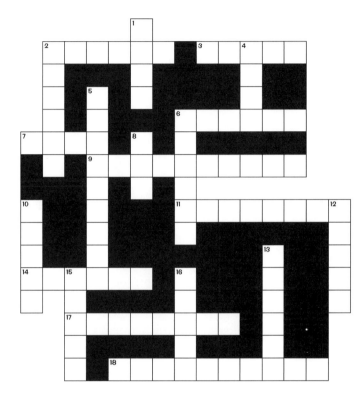

DOWN

1. Lucy's frozen purchase
2. "Bitter _____"
4. made a mess during tango
5. Ethel trims this
6. AKA Baby Chester
8. next to sugar, Cuba's biggest export
10. frequently caught in mid-air
12. pecan praline lady
13. Robert Taylor fruit
15. Lucy and Ricky's restaurant (abbr.)
16. "We've got sirloin, tenderloin, _____, rump; pot roast, chuck roast, oxtail stump."

ACROSS

2. Mr. Ritter's occupation
3. outgrew the oven
6. Lucy insults the chef when asking for this
7. Vitameata____min
9. Richard Widmark fruit
11. Lucy thinks this goes well with pistachio ice cream
14. escargots
17. hard to eat with, or Tennessee town (two words)
18. Mrs. Grundy's sandwich of choice

The Christmas Quiz

You'll find the answers to all fifteen of these Christmas questions by watching the "'*I Love Lucy*' Christmas Show." This episode, originally broadcast on Christmas Eve in 1956, was never included in the *"I Love Lucy"* syndication package and therefore never seen in reruns. Thirty-four years later, CBS rebroadcast the holiday show for the first time during the 1990 Christmas season. More than 40 million viewers tuned in that night, making *"I Love Lucy"* the most-watched program on network television for the week.

1 When Little Ricky asks how Santa Claus gets down the chimney, what is his mother's reply?

2 Fred and Ethel stop by with a gift for the Ricardos—a Christmas tree. How much does Fred spend on the tree?

3 Why does Fred end up buying a second Christmas tree for the Ricardos?

4 What does Fred pay for the second tree?

5 In addition to the second Christmas tree, what else does Fred return with?

6 In this episode, Lucy shows Ethel her favorite _____.

7 True or false: The Ricardos trim their tree on Christmas Eve.

8 Where is Lucy when she realizes she's in the presence of Santa Claus?

9 The "'*I Love Lucy*' Christmas Show" includes some memorable flashback sequences from other episodes. How many flashbacks are included in this holiday episode?

10 Which of these is not one of the flashbacks seen during this special holiday episode:

A Lucy tells Ricky she's going to have a baby.

B Lucy takes up sculpting.

C Lucy leaves for the hospital.

D Lucy sings in a barbershop quartet.

11 What do Lucy and Ricky tell the Mertzes they've bought Little Ricky for Christmas?

12 What does Santa Claus bring Little Ricky? Be specific.

13 While trimming the tree, Ricky sings a few bars of a classic Christmas carol in Spanish. Name the song.

14 What holiday ritual have Ricky and Fred been involved in year after year?

15 According to Fred, how many years has he been "putting up trees" with Lucy?

A twelve   **C** fifteen

B thirteen   **D** sixteen

The Anniversary Quiz

The following trivia questions are devoted to an event Fred Mertz once referred to as "an eighteen-year-old tragedy."

1 For Fred and Ethel's twenty-fifth wedding anniversary, what gift do Ricky and Lucy buy?

2 Which of these is not a title of an *"I Love Lucy"* episode?

A "Sentimental Anniversary"

B "European Anniversary"

C "Anniversary Present"

D "Hollywood Anniversary"

3 What significance has Grace Foster to the Ricardos' eleventh wedding anniversary?

4 Where do Fred and Ethel celebrate their eighteenth wedding anniversary?

5 In "The Anniversary Present," what three hints does Lucy leave in the kitchen for Ricky that she hopes will remind him of their upcoming anniversary?

6 In "Sentimental Anniversary," Fred and Ethel throw a surprise anniversary party for Lucy and Ricky. Excluding the guests of honor and Fred and Ethel, how many other people attend the party?

7 Lucy and Ricky's thirteenth wedding anniversary falls on a:

A Monday

B Tuesday

C Friday

D Saturday

8 True or false: Although the Mertzes have been married longer than the Ricardos, ironically, both couples were married on the same date.

9 Which anniversary do Lucy and Ricky celebrate in Hollywood.

A thirteenth

B fourteenth

C fifteenth

D sixteenth

10 True or false: In the very first televised episode of *"I Love Lucy,"* Lucy and Ricky celebrate their tenth wedding anniversary.

11 From which jewelry company does Ricky purchase Lucy's eleventh anniversary gift?

12 The year that Ricky gave Lucy stone marten furs, what did she give him?

The Vitameatavegamin Speech

How well do you know Lucy Ricardo's famous television commercial for Vitameatavegamin? Prove yourself a real *I Love Lucy* expert by completing the speech below.

"Hello _____.

I'm your Vitameatavegamin _____.

Are you _____, __-____, _____?

Do you poop out at _____?

Are you _____?

The answer to all your _____ is in this _____ _____.

Vitameatavegamin.

Vitameatavegamin contains _____, _____, _____, and _____.

Yes, with Vitameatavegamin, you can _____ your way to _____.

All you do is take a _____ after every meal.

It's ___ _____, too!

It's just like _____.

So, why don't you join the _____ of happy, _____

_____ and get a great big bottle of Vitameatavegamin _____.

That's Vita...meata....vegamin."

20 All About Little Ricky

Here's a quiz all about the first toddler of television comedy—Little Ricky!

1 What is Little Ricky's favorite bedtime story?
- **A** "Little Red Riding Hood"
- **B** "Goldilocks and the Three Bears"
- **C** "The Three Billy Goats Gruff"
- **D** "The Three Little Pigs"

2 Who's older: Little Ricky or Stevie Appleby?

3 Name the superhero who makes an appearance at Little Ricky's birthday party.

4 True or false: Fred and Ethel are Little Ricky's godparents.

5 Little Ricky's schoolteacher is Miss _____.
- **A** Campbell
- **B** Pringle
- **C** Duncan
- **D** Hines
- **E** Swanson

6 What is the name of Little Ricky's music teacher?

7 For his music school recital, how does Little Ricky's music teacher introduce Little Ricky's band?

8 What song does Little Ricky's band perform in "Little Ricky Gets Stage Fright"?

9 Who is Little Ricky's best friend?

10 When the Ricardos move to Connecticut, Little Ricky makes friends with the boy next door. What is the boy's name?

11 In which episode does Little Ricky laugh for the first time?

12 Name the Cuban nightclub where Little Ricky performs with his father.

13 Billy Palmer is one of Little Ricky's friends. What is Billy's mother's name?
- **A** Adele
- **B** Lillian
- **C** Phyllis
- **D** Daphne

14 In addition to Fred and Ethel, name a frequent babysitter the Ricardos call on to watch Little Ricky.

15 How old is Little Ricky when he enters nursery school?

16 In "Nursery School," Little Ricky comes down with _____ for the fourth time that year.

17 Who is Little Ricky's doctor?

18 When Little Ricky visits the hospital in episode 136, what room is he assigned?

19 Describe the first scene in which we are introduced to Keith Thibodeaux as "Little Ricky."

20 What is the name of the character Little Ricky plays in his school pageant, "The Enchanted Forest"?

21 What does Little Ricky suffer from in episode 156?

22 Lucy hopes that Little Ricky will grow up to be a _____, while Ricky would like to see his son become a famous _____.

23 In addition to "Little Ricky," pregnant Lucy considered naming her baby:

A James   **C** Roman

B Robert   **D** Henry

24 Little Ricky's first drum comes from which New York music store?

25 True or false: It was Little Ricky's idea to invite Superman to his party.

26 Little Ricky spends his third birthday at home with his grandma. Where are his parents?

27 What time of the day was Little Ricky born?

28 How many of Little Ricky's friends come to his fifth birthday party?

29 Name the doctor who delivers Little Ricky.

21 Fowl Play

1. According to Lucy, which of her friends laughs like a chicken?
   - A Grace Munson
   - B Marion Strong
   - C Carolyn Appleby
   - D Pauline Lopus

2. Where is Fred when he wakes up with a chicken on his chest?

3. Cousin Ernie breaks the Ricardo's television set while watching which "fowl" program?

4. In episode 171, how many baby chicks do Lucy and Ethel buy from the hatchery?

5. After Lucy ruins her chances of getting her Connecticut home in *House and Garden* magazine, Ricky jokes that they might have better luck making it in another periodical. Name it.

6. Name the episode that finds Lucy and Ethel riding on the back end of a poultry truck.

7. In episode 172, how many eggs do Lucy and Ethel attempt to sneak into the henhouse?

8. When Ricky accuses Fred of stealing their chickens, where does Ricky uncover the first stashed-away hen?

9. Name the musical band organized by Tennessee Ernie Ford.

10. Name the only *"I Love Lucy"* episode with the word "chickens" in the title.

11. While Lucy is supposedly on a hunger strike, where does Ethel hide a roast chicken?

12. Who are the two culprits responsible for all of the missing chickens in "Lucy Does the Tango"?

13. Complete the quote:
    Lucy: "...stop cackling. I've been waiting ten years for you to ____ ____ ____!"

14. According to Ethel, baby chickens like to talk about Fred. What do they say?

15. Which episode involves an exploding pressure cooker filled with chicken?

16. Fred claims to be qualified to be a chicken farmer because, "For years, _____ _____ _____."

17. What did Ricky say to Lucy the first time they met?

18. Five different *"I Love Lucy"* episodes included live chickens. Name them.

Funny Foursome 22

ETHEL

1. What role does Ethel play in Little Ricky's school pageant, "The Enchanted Forest"?

2. Ethel grew up in the Southwest. What was the name of the grade school she attended?

3. What's the story about Ethel's "Aunt Yvette"?

4. Which of Ethel's uncles is a retired butcher?

5. How old was Ethel when she married Fred?

LUCY

1. What instrument did Lucy play in her high school band?

2. In Cuba, Lucy unintentionally insults Ricky's Uncle Alberto. What does she call him?

3. When Lucy decides to change Ricky's wardrobe, who does she call to sell all of the old clothes?

4. In episode 103, why does Lucy dress up like Marilyn Monroe?

5. In what episode does Lucy take on the role of Sally Sweet?

FRED

1. What nickname does Fred give to Lucy and Ethel's women's club?

2. In "Lucy in the Swiss Alps," what confession does Fred make?

3. After seeing the disastrous results of her home permanent, what does Fred call Lucy?

4. Fred is originally from _____, Ohio.

5. Name the episode in which Fred loses a boxing bet with Ricky.

RICKY

1. As a singing matador, what is Ricky's first name?

2. What two places does Ricky want to visit while traveling to California?

3. "Tricky Ricky Ricardo" is also known as_____ _____.

4. When Ricky appears on *Face to Face*, what song does he perform?

5. Before leaving Hollywood, to whom does Ricky sell the car?

23 Episode ID

Here's a trivia quiz that tests how well you pay attention to detail. Try matching the episode details listed below with the title of the episode in which they occurred.

1. Lucy goes to bed with her foot stuck in a bucket.

2. Lucy gets sunburned.

3. Fred carries potted trees.

4. Lucy determines she's washed 219,000 dishes.

5. Lucy falls over a balcony.

6. The Ricardos and Mertzes are buried alive in an avalanche.

7. Clifford Terry produces a school play.

8. Lucy milks a cow.

9. Ethel and Lucy's "appearance" makes the newspaper.

10. Lucy brings a mule into the apartment.

11. Lucy impersonates a chair.

12. Ethel hides in a tree.

13. When Ricky leaves the apartment, Lucy calls an old boyfriend.

14. Lucy attempts the Sword Dance.

15. Murphy loses the fight and Fred loses the bet.

16. Ricky gets a haircut.

17. Lucy takes Rosa's place.

A. "Ethel's Hometown"

B. "The Fashion Show"

C. "The Girls Want to Go to a Nightclub"

D. "Ricky Asks for a Raise"

E. "Be a Pal"

F. "Lucy Is Envious"

G. "Lucy in the Swiss Alps"

H. "Ricky and Fred Are TV Fans"

I. "Lucy Is Matchmaker"

J. "Pioneer Women"

K. "New Neighbors"

L. "The Marriage License"

M. "The Passports"

N. "Lucy's Italian Movie"

O. "Little Ricky's School Pageant"

P. "Lucy's Bicycle Trip"

Q. "Lucy and Bob Hope"

18 Carolyn Appleby plans to impersonate Lionel Barrymore.

19 Ethel helps Lucy change a flat tire.

20 Lucy is reunited with her childhood doctor.

21 Lucy flirts with a store mannequin.

22 Ricky spends the night in the lobby of the Eagle Hotel.

23 Ethel becomes "Mrs. Miriam Chumley."

24 Lucy meets Phoebe Krausfeld's husband.

25 Lucy plays hostess to a "bleached blonde in wolf's clothing."

R "The Seance"

S "Lucy Visits Grauman's"

T "The Camping Trip"

U "Off to Florida"

V "Lucy Goes to Scotland"

W "The Star Upstairs"

X "Lucy and Ethel Buy the Same Dress"

Y "Lucy Changes Her Mind"

The Menagerie

1 In episode 103, Lucy's neighbor Mrs. Sawyer wants to audition her dog for Ricky's talent scout. What breed of dog does she have?

2 According to one of the Ricardos' neighbors, who's the "bee's knees"?

3 Which lion tamer once appeared at the Tropicana?

4 Seven *"I Love Lucy"* episodes contain animal names within their titles. Can you recall them all?

    A "Lucy's Show Biz _____ Song"

    B "Lucy Cries _____"

    C "_____ Fight Dance"

    D "The _____ Hunt"

    E "Deep Sea _____"

    F "Little Ricky Gets a _____"

    G "Lucy Raises _____"

5 While abroad, what did Lucy hope to eat with catsup?

6 True or false: Mrs. Trumbull shares her apartment with a cat.

7 In episode 31, what kind of animal is Ricky referred to as?

8 Name the fictional animal Lucy dreams of.

9 When Ricky puts Lucy on a strict schedule, he compares her to what kind of animal?

10 According to Carolyn Appleby, who is "the biggest female wolf in our crowd"?

Friends and Neighbors II

Can you identify these *"I Love Lucy"* friends and neighbors?

A_____

B_____

C_____

D_____

E_____

F_____

G_____

H_____

I_____

26 Sales Pitches

Identify the product or business name related to each listing below.

1. "It's so tasty, too!"

2. Its name implies quick cleaning.

3. You'd expect hot dogs and apple pie at this diner.

4. "12 more miles...10 more miles...just around the bend."

5. "...a great big bunch of gyps."

6. "The Inn on the River Out"

7. "The opinion of an average house-wife picked at random."

8. Brand of convertible taken on a Ricardo-Mertz cross-country trip.

9. "Our business is developing."

10. Bulldog _____.

11. "We do everything but eat it for ya."

12. Lucy calls this place "the watering hole."

13. Ginny Jones appears here.

14. Brand of washing machine pushed around by Lucy and Ethel.

15. Lucy and Ricky's diner.

16. "Laugh 'til it hurts with_____."

17. Lana Turner was discovered here.

18. "It slices, it dices..."

19. Dinner for a dollar.

20. Lucy saved forty percent on all she bought.

21. "People we place stay put."

22. These cigars are Uncle Alberto's favorite.

23. Ricky's movie studio.

24. Lucy and Ethel buy baby chicks from this establishment.

25. Lucy orders two sides of beef here.

Theme Song Sing-Along :27

The lyrics to the "I Love Lucy" theme song were heard only once during the show's six-season run on CBS. Can you sing the theme song? Fill in the blanks as you go and you could be the next bandleader on your block!

1 "I love Lucy, and ____ _____ ___.

We're as _____ as two can be.

Sometimes, we _____ but then; how we _____ making ___ again.

Lucy _____ like ____ ____ ____.

She's ___ _____ and I'm her ____.

And life is _____, you see.

'Cause I ____ ____, yes __ ____ ____, and Lucy ____ ___."

2 Ricky can be heard singing the theme song in which episode?

3 Ricky sings this special song he wrote for Lucy:

A at home

B in person at the Tropicana

C over the telephone

D none of the above

4 Who wrote the lyrics to the "I Love Lucy" theme song?

5 The "I Love Lucy" theme song was released as a 78 rpm record in 1953. Which well-known record company released the song?

28 In the Fifties

Can you identify which year each *"I Love Lucy"* event took place? Choose the appropriate letter for each event listed below. Your answers should reflect the year the event was first seen on television.

A =1950   **B** =1951   **C** =1952   **D** =1953   **E** =1954
F =1955   **G** =1956   **H** =1957   **I** =1958   **J** =1959

1. Little Ricky celebrates his fifth birthday.

2. Lucy and Ethel sell salad dressing on television.

3. Lucy writes *The Pleasant Peasant*.

4. The Ricardos and Mertzes are trapped in an avalanche.

5. Lucy gives her husband scalp treatments.

6. Lucy and Ricky celebrate their fifteenth wedding anniversary.

7. Ethel wants a toaster.

8. Little Ricky is born.

9. Lucy is held at gunpoint by a jewel thief.

10. Fred's old vaudeville chum, Barney, visits.

11. Lucy is reunited with her childhood doctor.

12. Ricky lands a summer booking in Del Mar, California.

13. Lucy impersonates Marilyn Monroe.

14. Lucy and Ethel carpool with Mrs. Grundy.

15. The Ricardos and Mertzes gather to "speak" to Tillie.

16. Fred sings "Oh, By Jingo."

17. The Ricardos appear on *Mr. & Mrs. Quiz*.

18. Lucy dreams about a two-headed dragon.

19. The Ricardos move into apartment 3-B.

20. Ricky's band rehearses in the apartment.

21. Lucy and Ethel vacation in Palm Springs.

22. The Ricardos and Mertzes travel home by train.

23. Superman is invited to Little Ricky's birthday party.

24. The Mertzes invest in oil stock.

25. Lucy loses her wedding ring.

26. Little Ricky learns to play the drums.

27. Lucy and Ethel find jobs at a chocolate factory.

28. Ricky judges a dog show.

29. The Mertzes move out of their apartment complex.

30. Ricky gives Lucy a string of pearls for their anniversary.

31. Lucy learns to jitterbug.

32. Ethel impersonates a medium.

33. Ricky and Fred are television fans.

34. Mr. Chambers becomes Ricky's new boss.

35. Lucy gives herself a home permanent.

36. Lucy, Ricky, Fred, and Ethel buy a diner.

37. The Ricardos buy a home in the country.

38. Lucy gets into a fight with a grape stomper.

39. The Ricardos rent their apartment to a murder witness.

40. Fred buys a Cadillac convertible.

41. Ethel meets Charles Boyer.

42. Sam and Nancy Johnson move into the Mertz apartment building.

43. Lucy and Ethel raffle off a television set.

44. Lucy goes to Turo.

45. Fred wears a frog suit.

46. Lucy meets Claude Akins.

47. Lucy gets locked inside a freezer.

48. Lucy is 33.

49. The Ricardos welcome Mrs. Porter.

50. The last original episode of *"I Love Lucy"* airs.

29 Members Only

1 Name the club to which Lucy, Ethel, Lillian, Grace, and Marion all belong.

2 In "The Hedda Hopper Story," Ricky performs poolside at a club function that Hedda Hopper plans to attend. What is the name of the club?

3 When Ricky buys his own nightclub, what does he name it?

4 Mrs. Pettibone and Mrs. Pomerantz are members of which organization?

5 True or false: Dorothea Wolbert is the president of the Ladies' Overseas Aid.

6 Lucy Ricardo and the Hudson twins win first place for their performance of "Ragtime Cowboy Joe" for which club's amateur contest?

7 In order to secure a nomination for club president, what does Lucy give Lillian Appleby?

8 Lucy and Ricky rehearse the tango in preparation for their performance at which club?

9 Lucy and Ricky perform "Songs and Witty Sayings" in a benefit show for a club Ethel belongs to. Which club is it?

  A The Happy Homemakers

  B The Tuesday Afternoon Fine Arts League

  C The Middle East 68th Street Women's Club

  D The Society Matrons of Manhattan

10 Mr. Littlefield ran which club?

11 While in Hollywood, Ricky plans a surprise anniversary party for Lucy at which nightclub?

12 In episode 69, Lucy and Ethel perform a duet for their club's yearly show. Name that tune.

13 True or false: Ethel wants to celebrate her nineteenth wedding anniversary at the Tropicana, but Fred wants to go to the fights.

14 Name the group of "outcasts" that Lucy temporarily joins on her birthday.

Incognito  30

Who or what is Lucy portraying in each of the pictures below?

A_____ **D**_____ **G**_____

B_____ **E**_____ **H**_____

C_____ **F**_____ **I**_____

In the Running

These questions relate to people who were responsible for "running" their own businesses—and the businesses they ran.

1 Who runs the charm school Lucy and Ethel attend in episode 81?

2 In "The Business Manager," who is put in charge of running Lucy's household account?

3 Name the husband and wife who run The Eagle Hotel.

4 Who took over the Tropicana after Mr. Littlefield left?

5 Name the fictional character Lucy created who ran "The Inn on the River Out."

6 True or false: Mr. Filo runs the employment agency that places Lucy and Ethel in jobs as candy wrappers.

7 One of Lucy's friends is married to a man who runs a television station. Name the friend, then name her husband.

8 Name the woman who runs a real estate business that is responsible for introducing timid Mr. Beecher to the Ricardos.

9 Al Hergasheimer is an old friend of Fred's. What kind of business does Al run?

10 En route to California, the Ricardos and Mertzes meet a real character who manages a run-down cafe where the only thing available on the menu is a stale cheese sandwich. Where are they?

11 Name the owner of the run-down cafe described in question 10.

12 Lucy buys modeling clay from an arts supply shop run by _____ _____.

13 Who ran the dress shop Lucy and Ethel purchase?

14 Who ran the dance class Lucy attends in "The Ballet"?

15 Name the company that runs the tour bus Lucy and Ethel take while in Hollywood.

16 Why did Lucy and Ethel run a raffle for the Ladies' Overseas Aid?

17 Signore Nicoletti runs which European hotel?
- **A** Hotel Grande
- **B** Hotel Dumonde
- **C** Hotel Royale
- **D** Brookshire Manor Hotel

18 Name the train company the Ricardos and Mertzes use to return to New York from Hollywood.

19 Name the mayor who runs the fictional village of Kildoonan.

20 In "The Handcuffs," where does Mr. Walters the locksmith reside?

32 Remembering Marion

Lucille Ball liked incorporating the names of personal friends into the *"I Love Lucy"* story-lines. In fact, one of Lucy's oldest friends, Marion Strong (they went to high school together in Jamestown, New York), was not only mentioned in several episodes, but an *"I Love Lucy"* supporting character was named after her as well. When the real Marion Strong married Mr. Van Vlack in 1955, Lucille began mentioning her friend "Marion Van Vlack" in select episodes. The real Lucille and Marion remained lifelong friends. The following quiz will determine how well you remember the television Marion.

1. True or false: Marion was a member of Lucy and Ethel's club, The Wednesday Afternoon Fine Arts League.

2. What is Marion's husband's first name?

3. The Marion Strong character was seen in all but one of the episodes listed below. Which episode?

   A "The Club Election"

   B "Lucy Is Matchmaker"

   C "Lucy Tells the Truth"

   D "Lucy and Ethel Buy the Same Dress"

4. What girls' school did Marion once attend?

5. Two different actresses played the role of Marion Strong. Name them.

6. According to Lucy, Marion's laugh resembles which barnyard animal?

   A pig

   B horse

   C chicken

   D goose

7. In episode 69, we learn that Marion was once a professional _____.

8. Lucy suggests Marion has poor taste in:

   A clothing

   B hats

   C handbags

   D makeup

9. While in Europe, what gift did Lucy buy for Marion?

10. Which William Holden movie did Marion see five times?

Out of Place 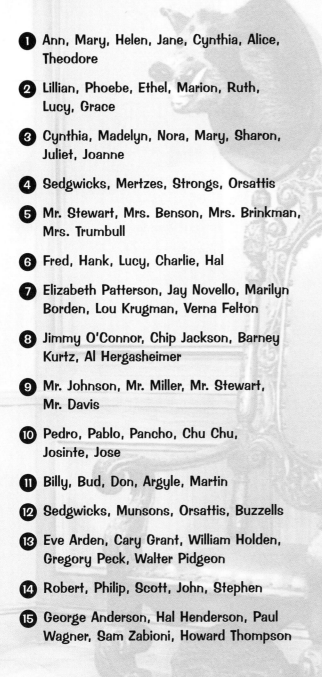 :33

Identify the person who's "out of place" and then explain what the remaining people have in common.

1. Ann, Mary, Helen, Jane, Cynthia, Alice, Theodore

2. Lillian, Phoebe, Ethel, Marion, Ruth, Lucy, Grace

3. Cynthia, Madelyn, Nora, Mary, Sharon, Juliet, Joanne

4. Sedgwicks, Mertzes, Strongs, Orsattis

5. Mr. Stewart, Mrs. Benson, Mrs. Brinkman, Mrs. Trumbull

6. Fred, Hank, Lucy, Charlie, Hal

7. Elizabeth Patterson, Jay Novello, Marilyn Borden, Lou Krugman, Verna Felton

8. Jimmy O'Connor, Chip Jackson, Barney Kurtz, Al Hergasheimer

9. Mr. Johnson, Mr. Miller, Mr. Stewart, Mr. Davis

10. Pedro, Pablo, Pancho, Chu Chu, Josinte, Jose

11. Billy, Bud, Don, Argyle, Martin

12. Sedgwicks, Munsons, Orsattis, Buzzells

13. Eve Arden, Cary Grant, William Holden, Gregory Peck, Walter Pidgeon

14. Robert, Philip, Scott, John, Stephen

15. George Anderson, Hal Henderson, Paul Wagner, Sam Zabioni, Howard Thompson

34 My Baby and Me

1. Name the twin boys Lucy once babysat.

2. As mentioned in "Lucy Hires an English Tutor," the Ricardos' baby is due in:
   - A December
   - B January
   - C February
   - D March

3. Five members of the Wednesday Afternoon Fine Arts League give Lucy a surprise baby shower. Name the episode.

4. In "No Children Allowed," which tenant reminds the Mertzes that the lease indicates "no children"?

5. Who is Lucy's baby doctor?

6. How old is baby Carolyn Bigsby when Lucy meets her?

7. Who is Bruce Ramsey's father?

8. According to Ricky, who is "the most beautiful baby in the whole world"?

9. Which of Lucy's old boyfriends has seven children?
   - A Paul Wagner
   - B Tom Henderson
   - C Howard Thompson
   - D George Anderson

10. What is the first name of Stevie Appleby's father?

11. To cure Mr. Ritter of his love for her, Lucy tells him that she has _____ children.

12. What childlike nickname does Lucy call Ethel in "The Kleptomaniac"?

13. Two "I Love Lucy" episodes include the word "baby" in the title. Name them both.

14. After _____ years of marriage, Lucy and Ricky are expecting their first child.

15. Returning home from Europe, what does Lucy dress in a baby bonnet?

16 In episode 80, Ricky misplaces the baby. What is to blame for his carelessness?

17 Complete the quote:

LUCY: "Well! How long has this been going on?"

RICKY: "What?"

LUCY: "They're _____ _____ _____ at Churchill Downs."

18 Fred's friend Barney has a grandson who lives in Indianapolis. What is the boy's name?

19 In the hospital waiting room, Ricky meets a man who's the father of six girls. What is this man's name?

20 Name Lucy's childhood babysitter who lived next door to her in Jamestown.

21 What childlike act does Pepito the Clown work into his nightclub routine?

22 True or false: While in the Ricardos' kitchen, Professor Falconi receives the news that his grandson has just been born.

23 Which of Lucy's friends gave birth to twins?

24 What song is Ricky singing when he finds out he's going to be a father?

25 As a child, Lucy was bitten on the ear by whose cat?

26 What is the fare for babies on overseas flights?

27 In Connecticut, Lucy has five hundred of these babies.

28 Evelyn Bigsby, and her baby, Carolyn, sit next to Lucy on the return flight from Europe. Name the actress who plays Mrs. Bigsby.

29 In which episode does Ricky sing "There's a Brand New Baby at Our House" while Fred and Ethel look on?

A "No Children Allowed"

B "Sales Resistance"

C "The Inferiority Complex"

D "Pregnant Women Are Unpredictable"

Starstruck

Anyone who knows Lucy knows that she is a fan of the stars. If you can recall all of her disastrous encounters with the celebrities she's met, you'll have a good chance at acing this quiz.

1 Name the movie star Lucy and Ethel meet poolside while in Palm Springs.

2 Upon checking into her Hollywood hotel suite, Lucy mistakes the house detective for which movie star?

3 Who is the first star Lucy spots in Hollywood?

  A William Holden

  B Eve Arden

  C Cary Grant

  D none of these

4 Who is the second star Lucy spots in Hollywood?

  A William Holden

  B Eve Arden

  C Cary Grant

  D none of these

5 Who is the one-hundredth star Lucy spots in Hollywood?

  A Robert Taylor

  B Cornel Wilde

  C Van Johnson

  D none of these

6 Lucy meets a famous comedian at Yankee Stadium. Name him.

7 Lucy hides under a dinner cart and hitches a ride to a fourth floor penthouse just to catch a glimpse of which movie star?

8 While on "The Tour," Lucy and Ethel see several movie stars' homes. In addition to the homes of Betty Grable and Harry James, Shirley Temple, Joan Crawford, and Richard Widmark, can you recall any two of the others?

9 At The Brown Derby, Lucy admires a drawing of Eve Arden on the wall. Lucy mistakenly assumes the drawing is a caricature of either _____ or _____.

10 Lucy attempts to be a "mirror" image of which star?

11 Who is the European movie star Lucy spots in Paris?

12 Who is "the dancing star"?

13 Which star does Lucy come face-to-face with at Macy's department store while she's trying out scuba gear?

14 While the Ricardos and Mertzes are in Hollywood, Robert Taylor is seen on two separate occasions. In which two places is he spotted?

15 To whom does Lucy say, "I bet you think we're crazy, huh?"

16 Which of the following stars doesn't Lucy meet while in Hollywood?

A Van Johnson

B John Wayne

C Rock Hudson

D Harpo Marx

17 Lucy spends the day at Schwab's drugstore after the hotel bellboy tells her that ____ _____ was discovered there.

18 What star carries Lucy away?

19 True or false: According to newspaper reports, Elizabeth Taylor was invited to Lucy and Ricky's fifteenth anniversary party.

20 On *"I Love Lucy,"* who is the last star Lucy meets?

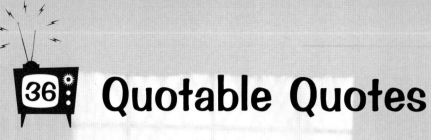

36 Quotable Quotes

Can you recall which *I Love Lucy* character said each of the following?

1 "Well done, Medium Raya."

2 "Cancel! Cancel!"

3 "Dilly dilly do."

4 "You're a good cook. You're the champion hostess."

5 "I love buttered grass!"

6 "Are you a-vampin' me?"

7 "All I know is that Columbus discovered Ohio in 1776."

8 "Oh, give her back her nasty old money."

9 "Nope. You can't get there."

10 "It's a poo-pah."

11 "Anyone who is the mother of a boy like that is all right with me."

12 "You're forgetting I'm the mayor!"

13 "...but you left before I had a chance."

14 "I'm just dying to see those lousy movies again."

15 "You didn't ask me."

On the Radio 37

In episode 32, "Lucy Gets Ricky on the Radio," the Ricardos' television set breaks down. And so Lucy, Ricky, Fred, and Ethel turn to the radio for some evening entertainment. Here are ten trivia questions devoted to this episode from "*I Love Lucy*"'s first season.

1 After the television set breaks, who suggests listening to the radio?

- **A** Lucy
- **B** Ricky
- **C** Fred
- **D** Ethel

2 What is the name of the quiz show the foursome tune in?

3 Mr. and Mrs. Findley are the contestants who appear on the quiz show the Ricardos and Mertzes listen to. What is Mr. Findley's first name?

4 Mr. and Mrs. Findley are asked three questions on this radio show: Who was the youngest man to be inaugurated president of the United States? What was the last state to be admitted to the union? What was the date of Lincoln's Gettysburg Address?

- **A** What is Ricky's answer to the first question?
- **B** What is Fred's answer to the second question?
- **C** What is Ricky's response to the third question?

5 True or false: For every correct answer the Findleys provided, they earned $100.

6 Can you recall the answers the Ricardos give to the following four questions when they make their appearance on the radio show?

- **A** What is the name of the animal that fastens itself to you and drains you of your blood?
- **B** What is a senator's term of office?
- **C** Why did the French people put Marie Antoinette under the sharp blade of the guillotine?
- **D** What did George Washington say while crossing the Delaware?

7 How much money do Lucy and Ricky win with their radio show appearance?

8 Who is the host of the quiz show?

9 According to a sign hanging on his office wall, what other radio show does this host emcee?

10 What is the first name of the quiz show host's secretary?

Facts on Fred

Fred Mertz fans, here's your chance to prove how much you know about Ricky's bald-headed buddy. Answer true or false to each of the statements below.

1 Fred was born and raised on a farm in the Midwest.

2 In "Ricky and Fred Are TV Fans," Fred enters a bet with Ricky for $25.

3 Fred is left-handed.

4 Fred was stationed in France during World War I.

5 Fred's hat size is larger than Ricky's.

6 Fred's mother lives in Ohio.

7 Fred was an only child.

8 In "Country Club Dance," Fred dances with Diana thirteen times.

9 In "Oil Wells," Fred originally has ten shares of stock and later sells five shares to Ricky.

10 Fred's father-in-law lives in New Mexico.

11 When Lucy takes up sculpting, Fred agrees to be her model.

12 Fred impresses his vaudeville friend, Barney, by pretending to be an oil tycoon.

13 Fred doesn't wear glasses.

14 Fred once worked at a diner in Indianapolis.

15 Fred was a lieutenant in World War I.

16 Fred plays the part of a turtle in "Little Ricky's School Pageant."

17 Fred plays the violin.

18 Fred suffers from seasickness.

19 While in Hollywood, Fred buys a motorcycle.

20 Fred speaks German.

Friends and Neighbors III 39

Can you identify these *"I Love Lucy"* friends and neighbors?

 A

 D

 G

 B

 E

 H

 C

 F

 I

A_____

B_____

C_____

D_____

E_____

F_____

G_____

H_____

I_____

40 "With this Ring..."

See how many of these matrimonial mind-benders you can answer correctly.

1 What does Lucy trick Ricky into believing is part of the "American marriage ceremony"?

2 What mistake does Lucy discover on their marriage license?

3 Which of Lucy's old boyfriends does Lucy claim "nobody would marry"?

4 True or false: Ricky proposed to Lucy in Greenwich, Connecticut.

5 What is the name of the book Lucy reads that persuades her to "be a pal" to her husband?

A *How to Keep the Honeymoon from Ending*

B *The Mockingbird Murder Mystery*

C *The Truth About Marital Bliss*

D *How to Have the Perfect Marriage*

6 Lucy and Ricky were remarried in the lobby of which business?

7 In what year did Ricky propose to Lucy?

8 On their honeymoon, Lucy and Ricky went:

A sailing

B skiing

C hiking

D swimming

9 Name the justice of the peace who marries Lucy and Ricky in "The Marriage License."

10 Which of Lucy's friends is responsible for introducing Lucy to Ricky?

"...Thee Wed"

Match the *"I Love Lucy"* wives with their husbands.

3. Carolyn Appleby   **A** Carl

4. Mrs. Guppy   **B** Mr. Meriweather

5. Phoebe   **C** Harry

6. Adelaide   **D** Norman Van Vlack

7. Madge   **E** Sam Johnson

8. Nancy   **F** Joe

9. Eleanor Spaulding   **G** Gordon

10. Grace Foster   **H** Charlie

   I Bill

   J Alvin Littlefield

Match the *"I Love Lucy"* husbands with their wives.

11. Bill Hall   **K** Emmy

12. Ralph   **L** Mrs. Ortega

13. Ben   **M** Lou Ann

14. Uncle Oscar   **N** Cynthia

15. Ricky   **O** Aunt Martha

16. Mr. Walters   **P** Lucille

17. Carlos   **Q** Minnie

18. Joe   **R** Betty Ramsey

19. John   **S** Edna Fisher

20. Elmo   **T** Abigail

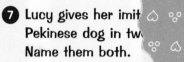

42 The Pet Departme

1 Match Little Ricky's pets' names in column A with the type of animal in column B. Need help? Watch episode 165.

Column A	Column B
Alice	frog
Fred	turtle
Hopalong	bird
Jimmy	goldfish
Mildred	puppy

2 Which of Little Ricky's pets fell out of the window?

3 Which of Little Ricky's friends gives him a puppy?

A Stevie Appleby

B Jimmy Wilson

C Bruce Ramsey

D Billy Palmer

4 Who tells Lucy, "That pooch has got to go!"?

A Ricky

B Fred

C Mr. Chambers

D Ethel

5 Name the grouchy tenant who threatens to move out if the Ricardos don't get rid of their puppy.

6 To protect Little Ri what does Lucy dc

7 Lucy gives her imit Pekinese dog in tw Name them both.

8 What is the name of Jin. Hudson's frog?

9 According to Ethel, what animal does Fred's mother resemble?

Instant Recall 43

Can you recall the episode in which the following situations take place? Match each situation with the episode title in which it occurred.

1. Fred sleeps with a chicken.

2. Ethel impersonates a newspaper photographer.

3. Two of "the world's greatest contortionists" appear at the Tropicana.

4. Goldblatt's Deli celebrates its fiftieth anniversary.

5. Lucy hides under a bearskin rug.

6. An uninvited guest ruins Ricky's maracas.

7. Lucy becomes Earl Robie's replacement.

8. Lucy talks about Ethel's rich Aunt Yvette.

9. The Tropicana is being repainted.

10. Fred buys pool cues.

11. Lucy lands a five-dollar-an-hour babysitting job.

12. Xavier Valdez replaces Ricky at the Tropicana.

13. Lucy's women's club celebrates its 25th anniversary.

14. Ethel and Lucy visit Minnie Finch.

15. Lucy compares men to goats.

16. Mrs. DeVries chats with Ricky on the telephone.

17. Lucy befriends a European boy.

18. Lucy brings an elephant home.

19. Ethel and Lucy practice curtsying.

20. Lucy sees green.

A. "Tennessee Ernie Visits"

B. "Ricky Sells the Car"

C. "Ethel's Birthday"

D. "The Amateur Hour"

E. "Lucy Fakes Illness"

F. "The Operetta"

G. "Ricky Minds the Baby"

H. "Charm School"

I. "Ricky's European Booking"

J. "The Kleptomaniac"

K. "Lucy Cries Wolf"

L. "Lucy's Bicycle Trip"

M. "The Tour"

N. "Ricky Asks for a Raise"

O. "Lucy in the Swiss Alps"

P. "Fan Magazine Interview"

Q. "Ricky Has Labor Pains"

R. "Mr. and Mrs. TV Show"

S. "Lucy's Last Birthday"

T. "Little Ricky Gets Stage Fright"

U. "Drafted"

V. "Lucy's Schedule"

W. "Lucy Meets the Queen"

X. "Lucy Gets Homesick in Italy"

Y. "Lucy Goes to Monte Carlo"

Your Name, Please?

Complete the crossword puzzle by identifying the first name of each character described in the clues below.

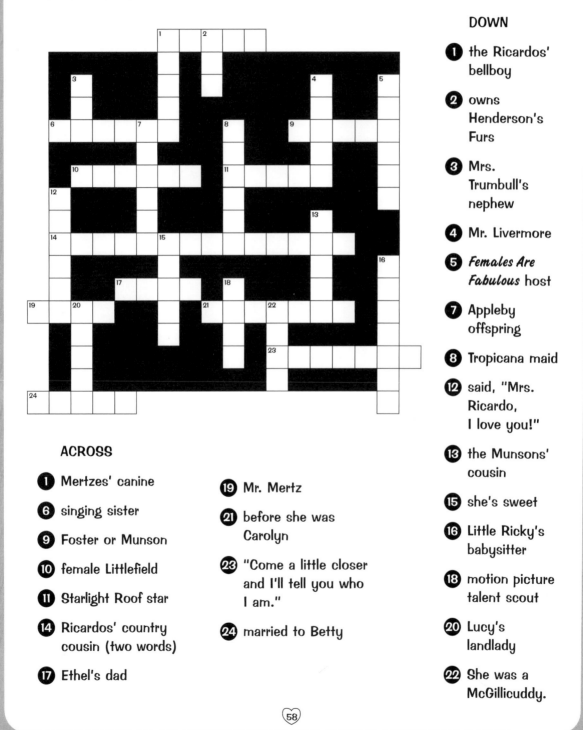

DOWN

1. the Ricardos' bellboy
2. owns Henderson's Furs
3. Mrs. Trumbull's nephew
4. Mr. Livermore
5. *Females Are Fabulous* host
7. Appleby offspring
8. Tropicana maid
12. said, "Mrs. Ricardo, I love you!"
13. the Munsons' cousin
15. she's sweet
16. Little Ricky's babysitter
18. motion picture talent scout
20. Lucy's landlady
22. She was a McGillicuddy.

ACROSS

1. Mertzes' canine
6. singing sister
9. Foster or Munson
10. female Littlefield
11. Starlight Roof star
14. Ricardos' country cousin (two words)
17. Ethel's dad
19. Mr. Mertz
21. before she was Carolyn
23. "Come a little closer and I'll tell you who I am."
24. married to Betty

45. Harpo Marx

Here's a quiz devoted to Lucy's famous encounter with Marx brother Harpo. All answers can be found by watching episode 124.

1 Lucy's friend Carolyn has rearranged her travel plans so that she can spend an extra day in California. Why does this upset Lucy?

2 Carolyn is on her way to _____ when she stops by for a brief visit with Lucy.

3 To trick Carolyn, Lucy impersonates several celebrities by wearing rubber face masks. How does she obtain the masks?

A Lucy borrows them from Ricky's movie studio.

B The hotel bellboy's friend at the masquerade shop helps her.

C Lucy buys them from a magic shop.

D It is never mentioned how she gets the masks.

4 Who is the first celebrity Carolyn is tricked into believing she's met?

5 What does Ethel "find" in this episode?

6 True or false: Lucy impersonates Bing Crosby.

7 In order to change into her movie star disguises, where does Lucy claim she needs to go?

8 What brings Harpo Marx to the hotel?

9 What song does Harpo play for Ethel and Carolyn?

10 Complete Carolyn's quote: "Imagine me being able to tell the girls back home that I caught a cold from _____ _____!"

11 Where is Little Ricky when Carolyn arrives?

A back home in New York with his grandma

B at the zoo

C on his way to California with Mrs. McGillicuddy

D It is not mentioned

12 What is the number of the Ricardos' suite at the Beverly Palms Hotel?

13 Carolyn left before seeing two celebrity look-alikes. Name the famous faces.

14 Where is Ricky when he asks Harpo to stop by and see Lucy?

15 One of the celebrities Lucy impersonates has laryngitis. That celebrity is:

A Jimmy Durante

B John Wayne

C Clark Gable

D Gary Cooper

The Telephone Directory

Match the *"I Love Lucy"* person or business with the corresponding telephone number as it would have been found if Lucy had checked the phone book. (Note: The scriptwriters gave the same telephone number to two different parties. The Mertzes and Ricardos were also given different telephone numbers on different episodes.)

1 Club Babalu

2 Eaton, Mel

3 Hotel Grande

4 Martha and Elmo

5 MGM Studios

6 MGM Studios: Mr. Schary's office

7 Mertz, Fred and Ethel

8 Nelson Photo Finishing

9 O'Brien, Tom

10 Ricardo, Ricky and Lucy

11 Zabioni, Sam

A PLaza-2905

B HOllywood 3-3449

C CHelsea 3-1068

D CIrcle 1-2099

E CIrcle 7-2099

F MUrray Hill 5-9970

G TExas 0-3311

H MUrray Hill 5-9975

I PLaza 3-2099

J GRamercy 3-8058

K PLaza 5-2099

L MUrray Hill 5-9099

M PLaza 5-6098

N SKyler 4-8098

47. The Puppy Puzzle

Using the letters assembled below, fill in the blanks in the right column to match the corresponding clues in the left column. Use each letter once.

```
B  B  B  C  C  C  C  C  C
D  D  D  D  D  D  F  G  G
H  H  H  K  K  K  L  L  L
L  L  L  L  L  L  N  P
P  P  P  R  R  R  R  S
S  T  T  T  T  W
```

1 Fred and Ethel's dog

_ U _ _ _

2 Richard Widmark's Saint Bernard

_ A _

3 *Is Your _____ Off His Rocker?*

_ O _ _ E _

4 The Ricardos were married at the Byram River _____ Club.

_ E A _ _ E

5 Little Ricky's puppy

_ _ E _

6 Lucy's possible ping-pong partner

_ O _ _ Y

7 Kind of cement

_ U _ _ _ O _

8 *Is Your _____ Off His Noodle?*

_ O O _ _ E

9 Ann, Mary, Helen, Cynthia, Alice, and _____

_ _ E O _ O _ E

10 Type of dog Cousin Ernie owns

_ O U _ _

11 Lucy: "Do you want to see my imitation of a _____?"

_ E _ I _ E _ E

12 He's no dog lover.

MR. _ _ E _ A _ _

13 *Is Your _____ Off His Trolley?*

_ O _ _ I E

14 Mr. Meriweather's cocker spaniel

_ I _ _ I E

15 Type of dog owned by Lucy and Ricky's neighbor, Mrs. Sawyer

_ O O _ _ E

Behind the Scenes :48

The nine people pictured below are among the many at Desilu who played important roles in the success of *"I Love Lucy."* Their names and their contributions are listed below. Can you match the names of these team players to their photographs?

1. Bob Carroll, Jr., scriptwriter
2. Irma Kusely, hairdresser
3. Bob Weiskopf, scriptwriter
4. Louis A. Nicoletti, character actor
5. Madelyn Pugh, scriptwriter
6. Elois Jensen, costume designer
7. Bob Schiller, scriptwriter
8. Jess Oppenheimer, producer, writer, director
9. Karl Freund, director of photography

49 ⚡ Friends and Neighbors IV

Can you identify these *"I Love Lucy"* friends and neighbors?

 A

 D

 G

 B

 E

 H

 C

 F

 I

A_____

D_____

G_____

B_____

E_____

H_____

C_____

F_____

I_____

Doctor's Orders

1 Choose the best match for each.

A Dr. Gettleman

B Dr. Rabwin

C Dr. Stevenson

D Dr. Spock

E Dr. Tom Robinson

F Dr. Joe Harris

G Dr. Humphreys

H Dr. Henry Molin

Psychiatrist

AKA Chuck Stewart

Diagnoses Ricky with morning sickness

Lucy's baby doctor

Says "nursery school does not take the place of home..."

Little Ricky's pediatrician

Author of *How to Keep the Honeymoon from Ending*

Diagnosed the "gobloots"

2 In which episode does Little Ricky receive a doctor's kit as a gift?

A "Little Ricky Gets Stage Fright"

B "Lucy and Superman"

C "Little Ricky Learns to Play the Drums"

D "The Ricardos Visit Cuba"

3 After Ricky won't let his wife perform in his new show at the Tropicana, Lucy decides to fake a nervous breakdown—with the help of a textbook on psychology. What three symptoms does Lucy acquire?

Multiple Mertz

Choose the best answer for each of these Mertz mind-benders.

1 In "Sales Resistance," what does Fred buy from the Handy Dandy Company?

A washing machine

B kitchen helper

C refrigerator

D Fred doesn't buy anything

2 As a cast member in *The Pleasant Peasant*, Fred becomes:

A Friar Flynn

B Squire Quinn

C Friar Quinn

D none of these

3 In "Fred and Ethel Fight," Fred moves out of his own apartment. Where does he go?

A YMCA

B a vacant apartment in his building

C clubhouse at his lodge

D the Ricardos' apartment

4 Which of the following characters does Lucy not persuade Fred to impersonate?

A a cab driver

B a painter

C a tavern owner

D a woman

5 Fred's mother lives in:

A Indiana

B Michigan

C Ohio

D New Jersey

6 Along with Ricky, Fred dreams up a juicy piece of gossip about:

A Grace Munson and the milkman

B Harry Munson and a female dancer at the club

C Mrs. O'Brien and the milkman

D none of the above

7 Fred owns a "Golden Gloves" sweater from:

A 1908

B 1909

C 1910

D 1913

8 In "The Marriage License," Fred has a friend at:

A the license bureau

B the courthouse

C the registry of deeds

D none of the above

9 At Coney Island, Fred once won a:

A teddy bear for Ethel

B cuckoo clock

C goldfish

D none of the above

10 What does Fred mistake for spirit gum?

A kerosene

B paint remover

C cement

D paint

11 What instrument did Fred play in Ernie Ford's band?

A washboard

B jug

C pots and pans

D kazoo

12 In which episode does Fred install chain locks on all the tenants' doors?

A "Equal Rights"

B "Ricky's Movie Offer"

C "Too Many Crooks"

D "Lucy Cries Wolf"

13 One of Fred's friends is a producer at MGM. What's his name?

A Nick Bascopoulis

B Frank Williams

C Carl Guppy

D Jimmy O'Connor

14 In "Second Honeymoon," how many years has Fred been married to Ethel?

A twenty-two

B twenty-four

C twenty-five

D thirty

15 While in Europe, Fred works for Ricky. What is Fred's job title?

A publicity agent

B band manager

C accountant

D none of these

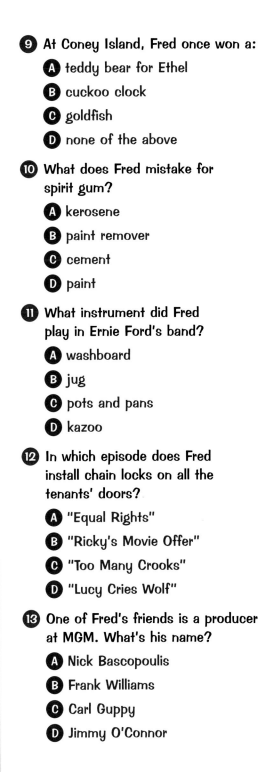

Everything's Relative

Match the name in Column A with the description in Column B. It's "relatively" easy.

Column A	Column B
1 Mrs. McGillicuddy	A has four sisters
2 Little Ricky	B son-in-law to Will
3 Ralph	C Mrs. Hudson's sons
4 Stevie	D also known as "Mother"
5 Joe	E Bruce's dad
6 Fred Mertz	F Sylvia is his sister
7 Weensy	G Ethel's uncle
8 Alberto	H her father's the sheriff
9 Mrs. Willoughby	I Ethel's godson
10 Diana	J Ricky's mother-in-law
11 Jimmy and Timmy	K Mrs. Trumbull's nephew
12 Eduardo	L Mrs. Appleby's son
13 Carlota Romero	M Barney's grandfather
14 Mrs. Ford	N brother to Ricky
15 Tom	O Ricky's uncle, the judge
16 Mr. Kurtz	P Harry's brother and business partner
17 Pablo	Q Mario's brother
18 Oscar	R she has twins
19 Jane Sebastian	S Harry and Grace's cousin
20 Dominic	T Ella Scott Porter's cousin
21 Roger	U Carolyn's mom
22 Angela Randall	V Ethel's fictitious aunt
23 Yvette	W Bill's wife
24 Mrs. Bigsby	X George and Ernest's brother
25 June Spear	Y daughter of a well-known cinema producer

Friends and Neighbors V

Can you identify these *"I Love Lucy"* friends and neighbors?

A _____

B _____

C _____

D _____

E _____

F _____

G _____

H _____

I _____

Name That Tune

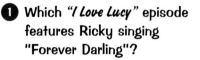

❶ Which *"I Love Lucy"* episode features Ricky singing "Forever Darling"?

❷ What song does Lucy perform with the Hudson Twins and their pet frog?

Ⓐ "I'm Breaking My Back"

Ⓑ "I'm an Old Cowhand"

Ⓒ "Ragtime Cowboy Joe"

Ⓓ "Ricochet Romance"

❸ In "Men Are Messy," Ricky sings a song that includes the lyrics, "Life can be a simple thing." Name it.

❹ What song does Ricky sing during his screen test?

Ⓐ "Babalu"

Ⓑ "Canta Guitarra"

Ⓒ "El Cumbanchero"

Ⓓ "The Straw Hat Song"

❺ Which song is not heard in the *"I Love Lucy"* episode that takes place inside a Tennessee jail?

Ⓐ "Birmingham Jail"

Ⓑ "Wabash Cannonball"

Ⓒ "Old MacDonald Had a Farm"

Ⓓ "Ricochet Romance"

Hide and Seek

❶ What is Lucy hiding in her mouth?

❷ Why is Lucy hiding her face from Ricky?

❸ What is Lucy hiding in her blouse?

❹ Name the Hollywood star from whom Lucy is hiding her identity.

The Numbers Game  56

Here's an *I Love Lucy* trivia quiz that requires knowledge of details you might have overlooked—until now.

1 When Little Ricky has to spend a night in the hospital, Lucy tries sneaking her way past the front desk so she can be with her young son. Which hospital room is the youngster in?

2 In "The Great Train Robbery," Lucy and Ricky travel in compartment A while Little Ricky and his grandma travel in compartment B. What's the problem with this arrangement?

3 When their daughter gets married, the Bensons move out of their old apartment and into another apartment in the complex. This move benefits the Bensons in two ways. What are they?

4 Place the Mertzes' tenants in the apartments they occupied.

1 Grace Foster   **A** 3B

2 The Bensons   **B** 1A

3 Albert   **C** 4B

4 Miss Lewis   **D** 2A

5 Sam Johnson   **E** 3D

6 Mr. Beecher

5 What is the only episode with a number in the title?

6 In "Lucy Goes to the Hospital," what hospital room number is she assigned?

7 In Italy, Lucy and Ricky are given room 47 at the Hotel Grande. Besides being on the fourth floor, what else can you say about room 47?

8 Which three apartments do Lucy and Ricky live in while renting from the Mertzes?

A 4A, 3B, 3D

B 3A, 4B, 3D

C 2A, 3B, 3D

D 3C, 3B, 3D

9 True or false: In "Sentimental Anniversary," Fred and Ethel reside in apartment 3C.

10 In "Lucy Is Matchmaker," Eddie Grant asks Lucy to meet him at his hotel room. What room number is Eddie staying in?

Grape-Stomping Stumpers

Her stint as an Italian grape stomper is one of the most memorable Lucy escapades. See how many questions you can answer correctly from this historic episode.

1 What is the name of the episode that includes the famous grape-stomping scene?

2 As the first scene opens, who is missing from the train car?

3 Where are the Ricardos and Mertzes headed at the start of this episode?

4 Why does Lucy impersonate a grape stomper?

5 Lucy's feet are compared to what type of food?

6 Name the Italian village where Lucy stomps.

7 What is the name of the Italian movie that Lucy hopes to appear in?

8 Name the famous Italian cinema mogul Lucy meets on the train.

9 Did Lucy go on a European bicycle trip before or after she stomped grapes?

10 In this episode, what is the Ricardos' hotel suite number?

11 What is the name of the vineyard worker who loses the opportunity to stomp grapes to Lucy and is instead sent to work in the fields?

12 In which year did this famous episode originally air?

A 1954
B 1955
C 1956
D 1957

13 What is the episode number of this show?

14 What is the name of the actress who wrestles with Lucy in the grape vat?

Friends and Neighbors VI

Can you identify these *"I Love Lucy"* friends and neighbors?

A

D

G

B

E

H

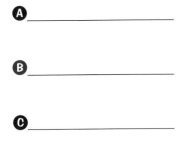
C

F

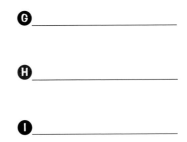
I

A_____

B_____

C_____

D_____

E_____

F_____

G_____

H_____

I_____

The Grauman's Chinese Theatre Quiz

These questions are devoted to the two-part story (episodes 128-129) of how a certain redhead manages to steal a pair of John Wayne's footprints from the floor court of Grauman's Chinese Theatre...and the hilarious escapades that follow when she tries to return them.

1 The story begins when Ricky, after completing the filming of his movie, returns to his hotel suite to find a surprise party waiting for him. What is the message on his cake?

2 While in Hollywood, Fred and Ethel are staying in the suite across the hall from the Ricardos. What is their suite number?

3 An ashtray and an old tin can are among the many souvenirs Lucy has collected while in Hollywood. Where did Lucy get the ashtray?

4 What is the significance of the old tin can mentioned in question 3, above?

5 When Lucy and the Mertzes visit Grauman's Chinese Theatre, which film is playing?

6 According to newspaper reports, approximately what time is it when Lucy and the Mertzes steal John Wayne's footprints?

7 Which John Wayne movie is plugged in both episode 128 and episode 129?

8 Instead of "Duke," what nickname does Fred call John Wayne?

9 In addition to those belonging to Trigger, whose footprints do Lucy and the Mertzes admire at the theatre? Need help? The first names of these movie greats are listed below; you supply the last name.

A Gloria _____

B Harold _____

C Tyrone _____

D Betty _____

E Joan _____

F Gary _____

G John _____

10 What is the name of the hotel beautician who does Lucy's hair?

A Peggy

B Irma

C Lou Ann

D Mary Anne

11 In order to persuade Ethel to help her keep John Wayne's footprints, what does Lucy agree to let Ethel do?

12 True or false: George is the name of John Wayne's masseur.

13 When John Wayne's footprints are found missing from the theatre the following morning, the news hits the papers. According to a newspaper article, a husband and wife are cited as witnessing unusual behavior by a redhead and a blonde prior to the disappearance of the prints. What are the names of the two witnesses?

A Mr. and Mrs. Walter Findley

B Mr. and Mrs. Irving Massey

C Mr. and Mrs. Paul Slate

D Mr. and Mrs. James Irvine

14 True or false: The witnesses are from New York City.

15 Where is Ricky when he finds out that Lucy has stolen John Wayne's footprints?

16 How many times does Ricky ask John Wayne to make a new set of footprints for the theatre's floor court? _____

17 The first set of replacement footprints are ruined by Lucy. Why does she smooth out the cement where the footprints were displayed?

18 The second set of replacement footprints are destroyed as well. Who's responsible for ruining this set?

19 Proving to be a good sport, John Wayne stops by the Ricardos' hotel suite and provides Lucy with a "six-month supply" of footprints. How many different cement slabs constitute a six-month supply?

All About Lucy II

Choose the best answer for each of these multiple choice questions.

1. Which of Lucy's old boyfriends is in the fur business?
   - **A** Howard
   - **C** Tom
   - **B** Harry
   - **D** Ted

2. In which episode does Lucy get "depalmed"?
   - **A** "The Star Upstairs"
   - **B** "In Palm Springs"
   - **C** "Ricky's Hawaiian Vacation"
   - **D** "The Dancing Star"

3. Lucy Ricardo once appeared on the cover of which magazine?
   - **A** *Life*
   - **B** *Look*
   - **C** *The Half Beat*
   - **D** *Photoplay*

4. Which magazine asks Lucy to write an article for publication?
   - **A** *Life*
   - **B** *Look*
   - **C** *The Half Beat*
   - **D** *Photoplay*

5. Which musical instrument has Lucy not attempted to play?
   - **A** piano
   - **C** piccolo
   - **B** saxophone
   - **D** drums

6. Lucy once claimed to be from which planet?
   - **A** Pluto
   - **B** Mars
   - **C** Jupiter
   - **D** Neptune

7. What song is known as Lucy's "Show Biz Swan Song?"
   - **A** "Sweet Adeline"
   - **B** "By the Light of the Silvery Moon"
   - **C** "Strolling Through the Park"
   - **D** "Carolina in the Morning"

8. While in Monte Carlo, Lucy wins big playing:
   - **A** blackjack
   - **B** roulette
   - **C** slot machine
   - **D** none of these

9. After _____ years of marriage, Lucy gives birth to Little Ricky.
   - **A** nine
   - **B** eleven
   - **C** twelve
   - **D** it's never mentioned on the show

10 In "The Dance of the Flower," Lucy played a:

A tulip

B petunia

C chrysanthemum

D dragon lily

11 To which Hollywood nightspot does Lucy go with Bobby, the bellboy, as her date?

A The Mocambo

B The Hollywood Bowl

C Ciro's

D none of these

12 Posing as Middle Eastern royalty, Lucy claims to hail from what country?

A Pakiraq

C Turkey

B Franistan

D Estiran

13 In "Lucy Tells the Truth," we learn the redhead's real age. What is it?

A 31

C 34

B 33

D 35

14 While returning home from Los Angeles via train, how many times does Lucy pull the emergency brake cord?

A three

C five

B four

D six

15 Lucy asks a stranger to buy one hundred of something. What is it?

A newspapers

C hamburgers

B cookies

D pencils

16 What did Lucy call little Stevie Appleby's playpen?

A a dungeon

C a hoosegow

B a cage

D none of these

17 Which two boys did Lucy date in junior college?

A Carl and Billy

B Kenny and Johnny

C Jason and Argyle

D Billy and Jess

18 In which episode does Lucy claim to hear a "little small voice"?

A "Oil Wells"

B "The Business Manager"

C "Ethel's Birthday"

D "The Ricardos Are Interviewed"

19 In "Lucy and Ethel Buy the Same Dress," where does Lucy buy her gown?

A Gimbel's

C Macy's

B Orbach's

D Prange's

20 As the Mertzes' maid, Lucy answers to the name of:

A Emily

C Beverly

B Bessie

D Belva

21 "Lucy Is Envious" of whom in episode 89?

A Jane Harcourt

B Cynthia Sebastian

C Jane Sebastian

D Cynthia Harcourt

61 Recollections of Ricky

These questions will test your knowledge of the man who loves Lucy.

1 In which episode does Ricky get promoted to manager of the Tropicana?

A "Ricky Asks for a Raise"

B "Lucy's Schedule"

C "The Publicity Agent"

D "Lucy Gets Ricky on the Radio"

2 In how many episodes does Ricky's mother appear?

A none   **C** two

B one   **D** five

3 Who thinks that Ricky is "the smartest, the handsomest, the most talented man in the whole world"?

A Lucy   **C** Ethel

B Peggy   **D** Mrs. McGillicuddy

4 Which magazine "visits an orchestra leader at home"?

A *Look*

B *Life*

C *The Half Beat*

D *American Weekly*

5 On which date does Ricky's screen test take place?

A September 17

B September 27

C October 3

D October 11

6 Name the television show on which Ricky appears while handcuffed to his wife.

A *Females Are Fabulous*

B *Guest Stars*

C *Face to Face*

D *Breakfast with Lucy and Ricky*

7 As one of the "four hot chicken pickers," what instrument does Ricky play?

A conga drum

B washboard

C spoons

D guitar

8 Ricky sang his first song when he was how old?

A four

B six

C ten

D twelve

9 In which episode does Ricky ride a horse?

A "The Gossip"

B "Pioneer Women"

C "Equal Rights"

D "Lucy and the Loving Cup"

10 What causes Ricky to explode in "Ricky Loses His Temper"?

A an overdrawn bank account

B his agent

C Fred

D a hat

11 According to Ricky, who is his best critic?

A Millie

B Mary

C Marie

D Maggie

12 How old is Ricky when he buys his first home?

A 25

B 33

C 34

D 36

13 Where is Ricky's band originally booked for the summer when their apartment is sublet to Mr. Beecher?

A Del Mar

B Vermont

C Maine

D Atlantic City

14 What gift does Ricky promise to his Hollywood maid?

A an autograph

B candy

C show tickets

D none of these

15 Lucy's mother once referred to Ricky as _____.

A Dicky

B Xavier

C Benny

D none of these

16 Which episode opens with Ricky reading *TV Guide*?

A "Ricky and Fred Are TV Fans"

B "Ricky Minds the Baby"

C "Ricky Loses His Temper"

D "Ricky's Hawaiian Vacation"

17 Which actress was being considered for the female lead in Ricky's film, *Don Juan*?

A Ann Miller

B Kim Novak

C Arlene Dahl

D Audrey Hepburn

18 What appliance does Ricky buy from the Handy Dandy Company?

A refrigerator

B washing machine

C stove

D shoe polisher

The Haberdashery

You might need to put on your thinking caps for this one—a crossword puzzle devoted to headgear!

ACROSS

3 affectionate mug (2 words)

4 The _____ Hat Salon

6 source of trouble in "Lucy Gets in Pictures"

8 The _____ Derby

9 Lucy's salad choice

DOWN

1 Lucy smashed his hat and ripped his raincoat.

2 She works at 4 across.

5 Richard Widmark's dog

6 Hollywood hat lady

7 "The _____ Hat Song"

Hooray for Hollywood

The Hollywood-based episodes of *"I Love Lucy"* are among fans' favorites. See if you can recall the details needed to answer the trivia questions below.

1. When Lucy is unsuccessful in her quest to go out to lunch with her husband and Richard Widmark, how does she end up spending the afternoon?

2. With which Hollywood movie studio is Ricky signed when he, Lucy, and the Mertzes head for California?

3. Name the two Hollywood landmarks that Lucy points out to Ethel in the opening scene of episode 114.

4. To what charity do the proceeds go from the Hollywood fashion show Lucy takes part in?

5. Where do Lucy and Van Johnson appear together as a dance team?

6. Whose Beverly Hills home does Lucy enter uninvited?

7. Who is Lucy's director in "Lucy Gets in Pictures"?

8. When Lucy "gets in pictures," who does she switch headdresses with?

9. While in Hollywood, Lucy talks Ricky into letting her buy a designer dress. Who is the designer?

10. What dollar limit does Ricky set when he tells Lucy she can buy a dress?

11. After Lucy buys her designer dress, she finds out that the wife of a famous movie star has the same dress in her own closet. Who is the star?

12. What does Lucy describe as Hollywood's "watering hole"?

13. Name the first two starlets the studio sends to the Ricardos' hotel suite to take pictures with Ricky.

14. What reason is given for shelving *Don Juan*?

15. While in Hollywood, Ricky hosts a television benefit for the Heart Fund. What costume does Ricky wear in the benefit?

16. Lucy and Ricky celebrate their fifteenth wedding anniversary in Hollywood. At which nightclub does Ricky throw their anniversary party?

17. Where does Lucy get her very own Robert Taylor souvenir?

18. Which theater can be seen from Cornel Wilde's penthouse?

19. In "The Hedda Hopper Story," Ricky gets a new publicity agent. Who is he?

20. Which of Lucy's friends from New York visits her in Hollywood?

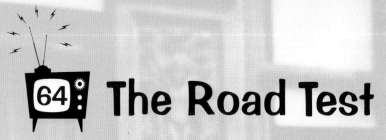

64 The Road Test

Below are twenty scrambled words. Each represents a place the Ricardos and Mertzes have visited. Can you unscramble all twenty words in the lefthand column without using the clues in the righthand column?

CLUES

1. ioho — It's round on both ends.

2. tornfebk (2 words) — rounded knife

3. liramola — city of the Texas Ann Motel

4. reqbequlauu — The people here never forgot Ethel.

5. doyoholwl — road trip destination

6. singlapsrmp (2 words) — tree type and season plus "s"

7. slirlehlyveb (2 words) — Lucy climbs a fence here.

8. nonldo — Ricky puts on a circus show here.

9. tonsdlac — home of the two-headed dragon

10. sraip — Lucy finds Charles Boyer in this city.

CLUES

11	zadliwnsret	avalanche country
12	yilat	Lucy gets homesick here.
13	melonotrac (2 words)	home of Le Grill restaurant
14	rolaidf	Lucy & Ethel's carpool destination
15	acbu	"I'm on my way to..."
16	tenitcnoccu	The Ricardos buy a home here.
17	amiim	Ricky & Fred judge a beauty contest here.
18	rout	grape-stomping village
19	lendnag	Angela Randall's homeland
20	wenemicox (2 words)	Mrs. Mertz' home state

65 ☀ Who Am I?

Can you identify the people linked to the claim made in each of the following statements? Some are characters from the show, some are actors.

1 Fred and Ricky impersonated my brothers.

2 I didn't know it, but Lucy Ricardo gave me a massage.

3 Mrs. Ricardo taught me to "side-step."

4 Lucy thought I wanted to blow up the Capitol but I'm just an actor rehearsing my lines.

5 My two sons wanted to burn Mrs. Ricardo at the stake.

6 Fred and I were once known as "The Laugh Twins."

7 I made money by buying Mr. Ricardo's old clothes from his wife and then selling them back to him.

8 I sold the Ricardos and Mertzes a diner.

9 My niece tried to market an old family recipe.

10 I played the part of a hollow tree in Little Ricky's school pageant.

11 I played both a second-hand furniture dealer and an English teacher.

12 Mrs. Ricardo and I won a ping-pong tournament.

13 Fred, Joe, and I helped Ricky get even with his wife when she posed as foreign royalty.

14 Lucy Ricardo raffled off a television set in my store.

15 My husband runs a television station.

16 I appeared in one special holiday episode and then disappeared.

17 I met Lucy Ricardo at Macy's department store.

18 When my partner, Hazel, became ill, Mrs. Ricardo took her place.

19 When the Mertzes moved to Connecticut, my sister was hired to manage the apartment building.

20 I was a redheaded hot dog vendor's middleman.

21 I'm Mrs. Ricardo's Hollywood hairdresser.

22 I used to write love letters to Ethel. Now I write for my hometown newspaper.

23 My wife and I moved into apartment 3D after the Ricardos moved out.

24 My old college roommate's cousin's middle boy visited Lucy and Ricky.

25 I was able to get Ricky a discount on pearls.

26 I went over Niagara Falls in a barrel.

66 First Name Basis

Fill in the blanks with the first name of the *"I Love Lucy"* character described.

1 Mrs. Mertz _ _ _ _ _

2 Lucy gave him dance lessons. _ _ _ _ _ _

3 The Spanish clown _ _ _ _ _ _

4 Mrs. Littlefield _ _ _ _ _

5 Beverly Palms Hotel bellboy _ _ _ _ _

6 He wrestled Lucy under a dining room table. _ _ _ _ _

7 Lucy and Ricky's mutual friend _ _ _ _ _

8 Ricky's cigar-smoking uncle _ _ _ _ _ _ _

9 Mrs. Appleby's first first name _ _ _ _ _ _ _

10 Mrs. Appleby's second first name _ _ _ _ _ _ _

11 Lucy's Westport neighbor and tulip gardening rival _ _ _ _ _

12 Mrs. Knickerbocker of the Wednesday
Afternoon Fine Arts League _ _ _ _

13 Lucy and Ricky's "cousin" _ _ _ _ _

14 Ricky's high school admirer _ _ _ _ _

15 Charlie and Carolyn's son _ _ _ _ _ _

16 Ricky's old girlfriend _ _ _ _ _ _ _

17 Mrs. Foster or Mrs. Munson _ _ _ _ _

18 Carolyn Bigsby's mom _ _ _ _ _ _

19 His middle name is Hobart. _ _ _ _

20 Lucy stomped grapes to impress this director. _ _ _ _ _ _ _ _ _

21 The star upstairs _ _ _ _ _ _

22 Ricky's movie character _ _ _ _

Palm Springs Puzzler 67

In episode 123, Lucy and Ethel vacation in Palm Springs—where they meet a "real live" movie star while basking in the sun. Find out how well you recall the ladies' trip to Palm Springs by taking this quiz.

1 In this episode, the Ricardos and Mertzes reveal some of each others' annoying habits. Match the person with the habit.

Lucy

Ricky

Fred

Ethel

A is careless with wedding ring

B "hogs" the bed covers

C taps fingers

D fakes coughing

E stirs coffee excessively

F is a noisy eater

G jingles keys

2 Which Hollywood movie star makes a guest appearance in this episode?

3 Name the movie that this guest star has just finished filming.

4 Why do Lucy and Ethel go to Palm Springs without their husbands?

5 Who does Ethel compare her husband to when discussing his bad habit?

6 While reading a magazine, Ethel finds a new recipe for chocolate cake. Which magazine provides the recipe?

A *Good Housekeeping*

B *McCall's*

C *Woman's Day*

D *Family Circle*

7 What is Mr. Sliff's wife's name?

8 What annoying habit did Mr. Sliff have?

9 Who does Lucy impersonate in this episode?

10 With the wives away in Palm Springs, what are Fred and Ricky looking forward to doing?

11 What does Ethel call Little Ricky in this episode?

A "Lovey"

B "Honey"

C "Sweetie"

D none of these

12 What unflattering nickname does Fred give Ethel in this episode?

Face the Music

Match the singer(s) with the song.

1. Tennessee Ernie Ford
2. Lucy and the Hudson Twins
3. Fred, Ethel, and Ricky
4. Mrs. Willoughby
5. Lucy and Van Johnson
6. Lucy, Ricky, and Bob Hope
7. Ricky and Lucy
8. Lucy and Ethel
9. Mertz and Kurtz
10. Teensy and Weensy
11. Ernie Ford and His Four Hot Chicken Pickers
12. Lucy, Ricky, Fred, and Ethel
13. Ricky
14. Dr. Peterson and Lucy
15. Ethel

A. "Friendship"
B. "Skip To My Lou"
C. "Ricochet Romance"
D. "My Hero"
E. "Y'all Come"
F. "Pass That Peace Pipe"
G. "Rock-a-bye Baby"
H. "I Love You Truly"
I. "Cuban Pete/Sally Sweet"
J. "Ragtime Cowboy Joe"
K. "Nobody Loves the Ump"
L. "Wabash Cannonball"
M. "Sweet Adeline"
N. "How About You?"
O. "Oh, By Jingo"

Friends and Neighbors VII 69

Can you identify these *"I Love Lucy"* friends and neighbors?

The Chicken or the Egg

In each group below, choose the *"I Love Lucy"* event that happened first.

1
- **A** Lucy portrays a witch.
- **B** Lucy portrays a wicked city woman.
- **C** Lucy portrays foreign royalty.
- **D** Lucy portrays a superhero.

2
- **A** Lucy and Ethel take up golf.
- **B** Lucy takes up sculpting.
- **C** Ethel takes up fortune-telling.
- **D** Lucy and Ethel take up basketball.

3
- **A** Lucy meets Rock Hudson.
- **B** Lucy meets Richard Widmark.
- **C** Lucy meets Van Johnson.
- **D** Lucy meets the Queen of England.

4
- **A** The Ricardos visit Cuba.
- **B** The Ricardos go to Hollywood.
- **C** The Ricardos go back to Greenwich.
- **D** The Ricardos go to Europe.

5
- **A** Lucy impersonates a hot dog vendor.
- **B** Lucy impersonates a chicken.
- **C** Lucy impersonates a cigar roller.
- **D** Lucy impersonates a ballplayer.

6
- **A** Lucy gets a Jacques Marcel original.
- **B** Lucy and Ethel buy the same dress.
- **C** Lucy and Ethel run a dress shop.
- **D** Lucy buys a Don Loper original.

7
- **A** Lucy and Ricky go skiing.
- **B** Lucy and Ricky go to Florida.
- **C** Lucy and Ricky go duck hunting.
- **D** Lucy and Ricky go to California.

8
- **A** Lucy climbs a brick wall.
- **B** Ethel climbs out on the fire escape.
- **C** Lucy climbs out on a ledge dressed as Superman.
- **D** Ethel climbs a tree with a raw duck.

9
- **A** Lucy is dressed as a bull.
- **B** Fred is dressed like a schoolboy.
- **C** Ricky is dressed like a matador.
- **D** Ethel is dressed like Santa Claus.

10.
(A) Lucy impersonates Gary Cooper.
(B) Lucy impersonates Walter Pidgeon.
(C) Lucy impersonates Harpo Marx.
(D) Lucy impersonates Clark Gable.

11.
(A) Lucy is "Lucita."
(B) Ethel is "Raya."
(C) Ricky is "Mickey."
(D) Fred is "Hippity-Hoppity."

12.
(A) Ethel sings "Shortnin' Bread."
(B) Lucy sings "Sweet Adeline."
(C) Ricky sings "The Lady in Red."
(D) Ricky sings "Cuban Caddy."

13.
(A) Lucy rides a tour bus.
(B) Lucy rides a bicycle.
(C) Lucy rides a horse.
(D) Lucy rides a tricycle.

14.
(A) Lucy eats a dog biscuit.
(B) Lucy and Ethel attempt to eat twenty-five pounds of cheese.
(C) Lucy eats a watercress sandwich.
(D) Lucy tries to eat a wax apple.

15.
(A) Lucy impersonates Harpo Marx.
(B) Lucy impersonates Tallulah Bankhead.
(C) Lucy impersonates Gary Cooper.
(D) Lucy impersonates Marilyn Monroe.

16.
(A) Lucy learns to drive.
(B) Lucy learns to curtsy.
(C) Lucy learns to give scalp treatments.
(D) Lucy learns to stomp grapes.

17.
(A) Lucy puts on a beard.
(B) Lucy puts on a fruit-bedecked turban
(C) Lucy puts on a tutu for dance class.
(D) Lucy puts on a slipcover.

18.
(A) Lucy reads *Is Your Spouse a Louse?*
(B) Lucy reads *Blood-Curdling Indian Tales.*
(C) Lucy reads *Abnormal Psychology.*
(D) Lucy reads *The Mockingbird Murder Mystery.*

19.
(A) Lucy says, "It's a moo-moo."
(B) Lucy learns of the boo-shoo bird.
(C) Lucy dances in Kildoonan.
(D) Lucy carries a papoose.

20.
(A) Lucy meets Ms. Jordan.
(B) Lucy meets Mr. Beecher.
(C) Lucy meets Mr. Stewart.
(D) Lucy meets Mrs. Grundy.

71 Superstition

1. Name the theatrical producer who attends a seance given by the Ricardos.

2. What is Ricky's astrological sign?

3. According to Ethel, which playing card signifies death?

4. In "The Seance," Ethel is introduced by two different names. Can you recall them both?

5. Ethel attempts to contact two spirits. The first is named Tillie. What is the first name of the other?

6. How long has Tillie been gone?

7. True or false: Ethel is a Leo.

8. According to Lucy, what does it mean if your palm itches?

9. According to Lucy, what does it mean if you drop a fork? Be specific.

10. What is Mr. Meriweather's astrological sign?

11. Match the numbers below to the most appropriate person:

    A Lucy   1

    B Ricky   3

    C Mr. Meriweather   5

    D Ethel   7

Star Search 72

More than twenty celebrities made guest appearances on *"I Love Lucy."* Can you identify the nine featured below?

A _____

B _____

C _____

D _____

E _____

F _____

G _____

H _____

I _____

Brand Name Match Game

Do you remember the name of the health tonic Lucy pitched in a television commercial, the name of the production company that shot Ricky's screen test, and the brand name of the washing machine that goes haywire in episode 67? See how you do with these brand name questions.

Match the names in Column A with the descriptions in Column B.

COLUMN A	COLUMN B
1 Handy Dandy	**A** health tonic
2 Johnson's	**B** delicatessen
3 Hansen's	**C** meat company
4 Le Grill	**D** mistaken for cat food
5 Phoebe Emerson's	**E** Italian restaurant
6 Eden Roc	**F** Maharincess Shaharazadi stayed here
7 Korwin's	**G** washing machine brand name
8 Pontiac	**H** hat salon
9 Martinelli's	**I** department store
10 Goldblatt's	**J** kitchen helper
11 Vitameatavegamin	**K** cabins and cafe
12 Aunt Sally's	**L** Fred's cross-country car choice
13 Aunt Martha's	**M** Ricky's cross-country car choice

14 Cadillac

15 Eperway

16 Phipps

17 Kramer's

18 Jeri

19 Dorrance

20 Speedy

21 Tony's

22 Canadian Allied Petroleum

23 Empire

24 Waldorf-Astoria

25 One Oak

26 Schwab's

N part of the Monte Carlo casino

O Hollywood drugstore

P Lucy is a substitute here

Q Connecticut hatchery

R charm school

S dress shop

T book publisher

U Florida hotel

V company that shot Ricky's screen test

W pecan pralines

X old-fashioned salad dressing

Y Kandy Kitchen

Z laundry

Trick or Treat

Treat yourself to this tricky quiz and see how many of these stumpers you can answer.

1. Who tricks Lucy into believing she has great sculpting talent?

2. In "Pregnant Women Are Unpredictable," Ricky offers to treat Lucy to breakfast in bed. What does he attempt to prepare?

3. In which episode does Lucy trick Ricky into thinking she has amnesia?

4. In "Staten Island Ferry," how does Fred trick the official at the passport office?

5. In "Lucy Raises Tulips," how does Lucy attempt to trick the garden club judges?

6. As a birthday treat, what does Lucy give to Giuseppe?

7. What does Lucy trick Pan American Airlines into believing is her son?

8. In "Lucy Writes a Play," all of the womens' clubs in town are having a playwriting contest. How does Lucy trick her club into allowing her to write the club's submission?

9. In episode 154, Fred treats Little Ricky to a day at the ballpark. Why is Fred so generous?

10. In "Lucy's Show Biz Swan Song," how does Lucy trick Ricky and the Mertzes into performing with her?

The Common Link 75

In each group below, choose the one word or title that doesn't belong. Then explain what the remaining words have in common.

1 Scotland
France
Italy
Monte Carlo
England

2 cat
dog
goldfish
lizard
frog

3 Procter & Gamble
Gulf & Western
General Foods
Ford Motor Co.
Philip Morris & Co.

4 *Be a Pal*
Females Are Fabulous
Be a Good Neighbor
Mr. & Mrs. Quiz

5 Carroll
Arnone
Pugh
Schiller
Oppenheimer
Weiskopf

6 Spock
Green
Gettleman
Harris
Rabwin

7 Jean
Mae
Louise
Roberta

8 "Lucy Does a TV Commercial"
"Lucy Plays Cupid"
"Lucy's Schedule"
"The Young Fans"

9 baseball glove
string of pearls
golf clubs
stone marten furs

10 "Ricky Needs an Agent"
"Bull Fight Dance"
"The Publicity Agent"
"The Fashion Show"

76 Undercover Ethel

Can you name Ethel's alter ego in each image below?

A _____

B ....

C _____

D _____

E _____

Eating Habits

1. While working on an assembly line, what food do Lucy and Ethel wrap?

2. In "Lucy in the Swiss Alps," what does Lucy try to conceal in her knapsack?

3. One of Lucy's aunts was well known for what condiment?

4. What are the four main ingredients of Vitameatavegamin?

5. What is Ethel's nickname for Jean Valjean Raymand?

6. In "Visitor from Italy," what does Lucy try to hide under?

7. While visiting her hometown, what delectable ditty does Ethel perform?

8. True or false: In "Lucy Hires a Maid," Mrs. Porter makes a peanut butter and jelly sandwich for Lucy's lunch.

9. In an attempt to meet Bob Hope, what does Lucy sell?

10. In "Lucy Gets a Paris Gown," where does Lucy hide the mustard?

11. In "The Business Manager," what does Ethel buy from the "redheaded green grocer"?

12. As heard in "The Diner," what menu item is Fred ordering when he says, "There's a gambler in the house!"?

13. In "Housewarming," Ethel reminisces about her childhood days in elementary school. What two desserts are incorporated into Ethel's grade school victory cheer?

14. What does Lucy crave at the end of "Ricky Has Labor Pains"?

Perfectly Puzzling

Using the clues in the left column, fill in the blanks in the right column.

1. He's a clown.

   P_ P _ _ _

2. "I've picked a peck of _____."

   P _ _ _ _ _ _

3. "Parker Preps Prod for Pitts _____."

   P _ _ _ _

4. She was Mrs. Trumbull.

   _ _ _ _ _ _ _ _   P _ _ _ _ _ _ _ _

5. English tutor

   P _ _ _ _

6. The Vitameatavegamin girl asks,
   "Do you____ ___ __ _____?"

   P _ _ P _ _ _   _ _ P _ _ _ _ _ _

7. Fred as a frog

   _ _ P P _ _ _ - _ _ P P _ _ _

8. Ricky works here.

   _ _ _ P _ _ _ _ _

9. They're a great big bunch of gyps.

   P _ _ P P _

10. He likes to sing and dance a lot.

    P _ _ _ _ _   _ _ _ _ _ _ _ _

11. Lucy meets Rock Hudson here.

    P _ _ _   _ P _ _ _ _ _

12. song performed in episode 59

    P _ _ _   _ _ _ _   P _ _ _ _   P _ P _

13. "Take Me Out to the Ball Game"

    _ _ _ P _

14. Ms. Emerson

    P _ _ _ _ _

15 opposite of "The Disagreeable King"   _ _ _   P _ _ _ _ _ _ _
P _ _ _ _ _ _

16 partner of Sticky Fingers Sal   P _ _ _ P _ _ _ _ _   P _ _ _ _

17 barbecue location   P _ _ _ _

18 originally titled *A Tree Grows in Havana*   _ _ _   P _ _ _ _ _   _ _
P _ _ _ _ _

19 played the saxavibatronaphonovich   _ _ _   P _ _ _ _ _ _ _

20 the musical playing at the Imperial   _ _ _   _ _ _ _
_ _ PP _   _ _ _ _ _

21 The Ricardos and Mertzes drive to Hollywood in a "brand-new _____ convertible."   P _ _ _ _ _ _

22 She had a crush on Ricky.   P _ _ _ _

23 Lucy's eleventh anniversary gift   P _ _ _ _ _

24 Pettibone and _____   P _ _ _ _ _ _ _ _

To Tell the Truth

In episode 72, Lucy tells the truth—and the result is classic comedy! How many of the following questions can you answer about this unforgettable episode?

1 Together, the Mertzes and Ricky bet Lucy that she can't go twenty-four hours without telling a lie. How much is the bet?

2 True or false: Lucy's true hair color is described as "mousy brown."

3 Can you recall what Lucy thinks of each person listed below?

1 Carolyn Appleby		**A** looks silly in her new hat
2 Ethel		**B** looks tacky
3 Fred		**C** has poor taste in decorating
4 Marion Strong		**D** is a coward
5 Ricky		**E** is a tightwad

4 What is Mercedes Minch's claim to fame?

5 At whose home do Lucy and her friends play bridge?

6 When Lucy attends a television show audition, she lands the part of the knife thrower's assistant. What is the name of the knife thrower?

Lucy Goes to Scotland

Disappointed that there's no time to visit Scotland on their European trip, Lucy goes to bed and dreams about what it might be like if she visited her ancestral homeland. Can you recall the answers to these ten questions without watching episode 144, "Lucy Goes to Scotland," one more time?

1 True or false: Lucy's ancestors lived in northern Scotland.

2 Who was Angus McGillicuddy?

3 Complete the quote:

Ricky: (laughing) "Angus McGillicuddy!"

Lucy: "What's so funny about Angus McGillicuddy?"

Ricky: "Oh, nothing, nothing. It's a very ordinary, everyday name. I know a hundred of them."

Lucy: "You should talk! I'll bet your great, great, great grandfather's name was probably _____ _____."

4 Who is the mayor of the Scottish village?

5 Which is not one of the musical numbers performed in Lucy's dream?

A "Dragon Waltz"

B "I'm In Love With a Dragon's Dinner"

C "The Last McGillicuddy Mambo"

D "Two Heads Are Nay Better Than One"

6 How does Lucy prove to the townspeople that she is a true McGillicuddy?

7 What is the full name of Ricky's Scottish character?

8 How often does the ferocious two-headed dragon eat a McGillicuddy?

A every twenty years

B every thirty years

C every forty years

D every fifty years

9 Who or what are Golspie and Ullapool?

10 In Lucy's dream, who sailed to Scotland with the Spanish Armada?

Musical Moments

81

Match each song title with the episode in which the song was performed.

1. "There's a Brand New Baby at Our House"
2. "Martha"
3. "Hinky-Dinky Parlez-vous"
4. "Y'all Come"
5. "Forever Darling"
6. "I'm an Old Cowhand"
7. "A McGillicuddy Is Here"
8. "I Love You Truly"
9. "Cuban Pete/Sally Sweet"
10. "We're Having a Baby"
11. "Sweet Adeline"
12. "How About You?"
13. "Down By the Old Mill Stream"
14. "Friends of the Friendless"
15. "Nobody Loves the Ump"
16. "The Mexican Hat Dance"
17. "I'm In Love With a Dragon's Dinner"
18. "Ricochet Romance"
19. "Man Smart, Woman Smarter"
20. "We'll Build a Bungalow"
21. "Rock-a-bye Baby"
22. "Shine On, Harvest Moon"
23. "*I Love Lucy*" theme song
24. "Lady of Spain"
25. "Pass That Peace Pipe"

A. "The Diet"
B. "Tennessee Bound"
C. "Lucy Is Enceinte"
D. "Lucy and Bob Hope"
E. "Lucy's Show Biz Swan Song"
F. "Sales Resistance"
G. "Lucy Goes to a Rodeo"
H. "Ricky's European Booking"
I. "Ricky's Life Story"
J. "The Ballet"
K. "Lucy's Last Birthday"
L. "The Benefit"
M. "Breaking the Lease"
N. "Lucy Goes to Scotland"
O. "The Indian Show"
P. "The Passports"
Q. "Home Movies"
R. "Dancing Star"
S. "The Marriage License"
T. "Tennessee Ernie Hangs On"
U. "Ragtime Band"

Complete the Quote

1 "You're nurturing two vipers in your _____ _____."
—Lucy, warning Ethel about the Mertzes' new tenants

2 "City woman! Where are you at, you little _____!"
—Cousin Ernie, in search of the wicked city woman

3 "You become a _____ ____."
—Lucy, scolding Walter Reilly

4 "I've got her jumping around like a _____ ____."
—Ricky, boasting to Fred about his success in keeping Lucy on schedule

5 "Some people are cut out for champagne and caviar.
I'm more the ____ and _____ type."
—Lucy, explaining why she isn't cut out to have a maid

6 "We have become stuffy, moldy, and musty.
We are _____-_____ in a pool of _____."
—Lucy, justifying the need for a vacation from marriage

7 "Ethel has the habit of _____ ____ ___ _____ until it gets sickening."
—Ricky, commenting on one of Ethel's bad habits

8 "If I wasn't so sick and tired of him, I'd, I'd _____ ____."
—Lucy, speaking about Cousin Ernie's visit

9 "Come to think of it, she does have the biggest _____ I've ever seen."
—Lucy, commenting on Ethel's appearance

83 Take a Number

1 When returning home from Europe, what number is assigned to the Ricardos and Mertzes airline flight?

2 In episode 87, Ricky finds a "bonus buck"—a dollar bill with a specific serial number. What serial number designates the dollar bill a "bonus buck"?

3 How many ice cubes does Lucy think it takes to keep a tuna cool?

4 In "First Stop," the Ricardos and Mertzes spend a night in a rickety old cabin. How much, per couple, do they pay?

5 Lucy wears a Cleveland Indians jersey when posing as a baseball player in an attempt to meet Bob Hope. What number is on the jersey she wears?

6 In "Lucy Does the Tango," Lucy trades five hundred baby chicks for how many hens?

7 How old was Lucy when she married Ricky?

8 The Ricardos purchase their Connecticut home from Joe and Eleanor Spaulding. How many years had the Spauldings lived there?

9 In "Breaking the Lease," how many months are left on the Ricardo's lease?

10 In "The Diet," we learn that since she's been married, Lucy has gained some weight. How many pounds?

11 How many cakes of yeast does Lucy use when making her memorable loaf of bread?

12 In "The Sublease," how much does Mr. Beecher pay per month to sublet the Ricardos' apartment?

13 What is Bobby's response to Lucy when she asks, "What room is my husband in?"

14 What is the population of cousin Ernie's hometown, Bent Fork, Tennessee?

15 What is the alcohol content of Vitameatavegamin?

16 In "Ricky Asks for a Raise," how many tables does the Tropicana have?

17 How many pounds of beef does Lucy order in "The Freezer"?

18 Lucy and Ethel buy a tuna here.

19 In "Lucy Gets Chummy with the Neighbors," how much does Lucy spend on new furniture?

20 In "Lucy Goes to Monte Carlo," Lucy wins 875,000 francs at the roulette table by selecting two numbers. What are they?

Can you identify these *"I Love Lucy"* friends and neighbors?

A_____

B_____

C_____

D_____

E_____

F_____

G_____

H_____

I_____

The Truth About Ethel

Here's your chance to show what you know about that lovely landlady from East 68th Street. Answer true or false to each of the following claims.

1. Ethel is originally from Arizona.

2. Ethel's middle name is Louise.

3. When Ethel married Fred, they eloped.

4. Knitting is one of Ethel's hobbies.

5. Ethel is godmother to Little Ricky.

6. Ethel has been known to use her pass key to snoop on new tenants while they're away.

7. In "The Million-Dollar Idea," Ethel sells salad dressing for forty cents per pint.

8. Emmy and Martha are names of two of Ethel's aunts.

9. Ethel was raised on a ranch.

10. Ethel speaks Italian.

11. Ethel's maiden name is Porter.

12. Ethel was once a vaudeville performer.

13. Ethel can tell fortunes with playing cards.

14. Ethel was once mistaken for a crook known as "Sticky Fingers Sal."

15. Ethel once held the title of "Miss New Mexico."

16. Ethel and Betty Foster attended the same grade school.

17. Ethel is superstitious.

18. In "Ethel's Hometown," Ethel's middle name is Mae.

19. The Mertz apartment building is in Ethel's name.

20. According to Ethel, Grace Munson is the "Elsa Maxwell of Westport."

The Fashion Show

86

While visiting Don Loper's salon, Lucy manages to get herself invited to take part in a special charity fashion show. Here are ten questions from the episode showcasing Lucy's stint as a Hollywood model.

1. The models in the fashion show are wives of Hollywood movie stars. From whom does Lucy learn about the event?

2. What is the price of the dress Lucy purchases from the Loper salon?

3. While Lucy is getting sunburned, where are Fred and Ethel?

4. Which of her friends does Lucy hope to make jealous when she returns home with a Don Loper original?

5. What size dress does Lucy ask to see while visiting the salon?

6. In two words, describe the Don Loper outfit Lucy models.

7. In this episode, how does Lucy describe both her own and Ethel's complexions?

8. Name the charity that benefits from the proceeds of the fashion show Don Loper hosts.

9. Which Hollywood star's wife does not appear in the fashion show?
   A. Van Heflin
   B. William Holden
   C. Clark Gable
   D. Forrest Tucker

10. Name the Hollywood wives pictured below with Don Loper (from left to right).

Critic's Choice

In each of the following excerpts, identify which *"I Love Lucy"* episode is being reviewed.

1 "Ball's portrayal of Lucy Ricardo's impersonation of movie star Marilyn Monroe is one of this episode's highlights..."

2 "It's a classic case of mistaken identity and some all-too-often cord tugging..."

3 "The climax of the show is the appearance of a baby elephant, which comes as a real surprise and carries the audience to hilarity..."

4 "Women all over the world can relate to Lucy's annual aging dilemma..."

5 "With lollipop in hand, Frawley's unexpected performance of a school boy catches the audience off guard and leaves them in stitches..."

6 "Ball and Arnaz convincingly apply the aging process to their characters in a successful attempt at scaring away their youthful admirers..."

7 "A hilarious comedy of errors ensues when a letter from the government starts the whole ball of yarn rolling..."

8 "Ball and Vance's dialogue is so convincing, you'd think they'd just crawled out of a space ship..."

9 "Fists fly and books bounce in this brilliantly written episode that leaves the four stars visibly disfigured..."

10 "As a starstruck Lucy Ricardo, Lucille Ball proves that even dining can be disastrous..."

88. Do You Know?

Using the numbered clues at the bottom of the page, fill in the blanks with the names of people, places, and things associated with "*I Love Lucy*."

Clues:

1 D O _ _ _ _ _

1 Ricky goes to Hollywood to star in this movie.

2 _ _ _ D O _ _ _ _

2 Lucy's dreamy village

3 _ _ _ D O _

3 foreign city where Ricky presents a circus-themed revue

4 _ _ _ _ _ _ _ _ _ _ D O _ _ _ _ _ _ _

4 Lucy, the Mertzes, and Mrs. McGillicuddy are members.

5 _ _ _ _ D O _ _ _ _ _ _ _

5 Lucy mistakes this for spirit gum.

6 D O _

6 the source of controversy in episode 165

7 _ _ _ _ _ _ _ D O _

7 He was Mr. Littlefield.

8 _ _ _ D O _ _ _ _ _ _

8 Lucy used this as a hiding place.

9 _ _ _ _ _ _ D O _ _ _ _ _ _ _

9 The Ricardos' dedicate a statue for this event.

10 D O _ _ _ _ _ _ _ _ _ _ _

10 Lucy's childhood physician

11 D O _   _ _ _ _ _

11 Lucy takes part in this designer's fashion show.

12 D O _ _ _ _

12 Lucy gets caught in a starch vat because of this.

13 D O _ _ _ _ _ _   _ _ _ _ _ _

13 She's a president.

14 _ _ _ D O _

14 Tropicana show theme the night Little Ricky is born.

15 _ _ _   &   D O _ _ _ _ _

15 Carter and Cooke

16 _ _ _ _   _ _ _ _ _ D O

16 formerly McGillicuddy

17 D O _ _ _ _ _ _   _ _ _   _ _ _ _ _ _ _

17 Lucy's publisher

18 _ _ _ _ D O _ _

18 "That's _____!"

19 _ _ _ D O _   _ _ _ _ _ _ _ _

19 Ricky performs here for the Queen of England.

20 D O _ _   _ _ _ _ _ _

20 MGM Studios chief

21 D O _ _ _ _

21 Lucy gets caught doing this in "Home Movie".

22 _ _ _   D O _   _ _ _ D O _

22 Lucy meets Bob Hope by pretending to be this.

23 _ _ _ _ _   _ _ _ _ _ _ _   D O _ _ _ _ _ _

23 substituted this for their car

24 _ _ _ D O _ _ _ _

24 Mario's occupation

25 D O _ _ _ _ _ _ _ _

25 A twenty-inch television is delivered here.

That Never Happened!

In each group below, choose the *"I Love Lucy"* event that never was.

1
- **A** Lucy buys a freezer.
- **B** Lucy buys a vacuum cleaner.
- **C** Lucy buys a doctor's kit.
- **D** Lucy buys a washing machine.

2
- **A** Little Ricky gets a lizard.
- **B** Little Ricky gets a hamster.
- **C** Little Ricky gets goldfish.
- **D** Little Ricky gets a bunny.

3
- **A** Lucy goes to Monte Carlo.
- **B** Lucy goes to Paris.
- **C** Lucy goes to Scotland.
- **D** Lucy goes to Florida.

4
- **A** Lucy gets drunk on health tonic.
- **B** Lucy gets handcuffed.
- **C** Lucy gets thrown in a Kentucky jail.
- **D** Lucy gets locked in a trunk.

5
- **A** Lucy sits on a ledge.
- **B** Lucy bird-sits.
- **C** Lucy sits in wet cement.
- **D** Lucy babysits twins.

6
- **A** Ethel sells salad dressing with Lucy.
- **B** Lucy sells raffle tickets.
- **C** Lucy sells one-cent hamburgers.
- **D** Ethel sells beef.

7
- **A** Ricky performs with Bob Hope.
- **B** Fred meets Percy Livermore.
- **C** Lucy crushes John Wayne's hat.
- **D** Ethel touches Eve Arden.

8
- **A** The Ricardos visit Cuba.
- **B** Fred and Ethel visit Jamestown, New York.
- **C** Lucy goes to Hawaii.
- **D** The Mertzes vacation in Florida.

9
- **A** Fred is a drummer.
- **B** Fred is a bell ringer.
- **C** Fred is a dragon.
- **D** Fred is a cabdriver.

10
- **A** Carolyn meets Van Johnson.
- **B** Lucy meets Robert Taylor.
- **C** Ethel meets William Holden.
- **D** Fred meets John Wayne.

Lucy's Loving Cup

Here are ten teasers based on episode 164.

 Why does Lucy put the loving cup on her head?

 With the loving cup stuck on her head, Lucy insults a police officer. At which subway stop does this occur?

3 Ricky plans to present the loving cup at a banquet in honor of jockey Johnny Longden. What is the trophy for?

4 Lucy buys a new dress for the banquet. How much does the dress cost?

5 According to this episode, how many races has Johnny Longden won?

6 Johnny Longden's wife appears in this episode. What is her first name?

7 While on the subway, Lucy wears a large veil to hide the loving cup. When and where does it fall off?

8 At which stop do Lucy and Ethel get separated?

9 Ethel offers to accompany Lucy on the subway, but refuses to go until she's able to do what?

10 At the beginning of this episode Lucy brings home a new hat. Upon seeing the hat, to what does Ricky compare it?

91 Lasting Impressions

1. What is the last name of Lucy's wealthy ex-school chum in episode 89?

2. What is found in the last scene of the last episode of *I Love Lucy*?

3. True or false: Ricky sings the show's theme song in "Lucy's Last Birthday."

4. What occurs in the last moments of the famous Vitameatavegamin episode?

5. In "L.A. at Last," what costume does Ricky wear while in Bill Sherman's office?

6. Name the clown whose impression of a crying baby can be seen in "Lucy's Show Biz Swan Song."

7. In "Paris at Last," which scriptwriter can be seen in the sidewalk café scene?

8. Lucy makes a bad first impression when she causes Ricky to be late for a dinner appointment with the new boss of the Tropicana. In which episode does this event take place?

   A "Ricky Asks for a Raise"   C "Job Switching"

   B "The Amateur Hour"   D "Lucy's Schedule"

Lyrical Lucy

Can you identify the song titles from the selected lyrical snippets listed below?

1 "...in the parlor, in the hall, every picture on the wall seems to know because they all wear a smile..."

2 "When I play the maracas I go chick, chicky boom, chick chicky boom..."

3 "They warned me when you kissed me, your love would ricochet..."

4 "While pushing that carriage, how happy we'll be..."

5 "I'll be your true love forever and forever..."

6 "Right back where I started from..."

7 "That's right, the woman is...."

8 "...and when we're married, happy we'll be... underneath the bamboo tree..."

9 "I'm in love, I'm in love, I'm in love, I'm in love, I'm in love..."

10 "Lucy kisses like no one can. She's my missus and I'm her man. And life is heaven you see..."

93 Final Thoughts

In each group below, select the event that occurred last.

1. **A** Lucy raises chickens.
   B Lucy raises bread.
   C Lucy raises tulips.

2. **A** Lucy writes a novel.
   B Lucy writes a play.
   C Lucy writes an operetta.

3. **A** Lucy meets Johnny Longden.
   B Lucy meets Jimmy Demaret.
   C Lucy Meets Claude Akins.

4. **A** Little Ricky learns to play the drums.
   B Little Ricky stars in a school pageant.
   C Little Ricky gets stage fright.

5. **A** Lucy buys two sides of beef.
   B Lucy buys a Don Loper original.
   C Lucy buys fifty pounds of modeling clay.

6. **A** The Ricardos get a visitor from Italy.
   B Superman visits the Ricardos.
   C The Ricardos visit Cuba.

7. **A** "Lucy Is Matchmaker"
   B "Lucy Plays Cupid"
   C "The Matchmaker"

8. **A** Lucy raps a talent scout over the head.
   B Lucy and Ethel wrap chocolates.
   C Lucy raps two actors over the head in her apartment.

9. **A** Cynthia Harcourt stops by the Ricardos' apartment.
   B Eleanor Harris stops by the Ricardos' apartment.
   C Bennett Green stops by the Ricardos' apartment.

10
Ⓐ Lucy hides an elephant.

Ⓑ Lucy hides her living room furniture.

Ⓒ Lucy hides a clock in her coat.

11
Ⓐ Ricky dresses as a Scotsman.

Ⓑ Ricky dresses as a voodoo doctor.

Ⓒ Ricky dresses as an Indian.

12
Ⓐ Ricky sells a car.

Ⓑ Ethel borrows some luggage.

Ⓒ Fred buys a motorcycle.

13
Ⓐ Lucy worries about Diana Jordan.

Ⓑ Lucy worries about Carlota Romero.

Ⓒ Lucy worries about Peggy Dawson.

14
Ⓐ The Ricardos and Mertzes visit Monte Carlo.

Ⓑ The Ricardos and Mertzes attend a rodeo.

Ⓒ The Ricardos and Mertzes go to Switzerland.

15
Ⓐ "Ricky's Hawaiian Vacation"

Ⓑ "California, Here We Come!"

Ⓒ "Vacation from Marriage"

16
Ⓐ Lucy and Ethel play basketball.

Ⓑ Lucy and Ethel go fishing.

Ⓒ Lucy and Ethel take up golf.

17
Ⓐ "Ricky Has Labor Pains"

Ⓑ "Lucy Gets Homesick in Italy"

Ⓒ "Lucy Fakes Illness"

18
Ⓐ Lucy sells beef.

Ⓑ Lucy sells salad dressing.

Ⓒ Lucy sells raffle tickets.

19
Ⓐ Lucy dances with Van Johnson.

Ⓑ Lucy dances in a bull costume.

Ⓒ Lucy dances with Arthur Morton.

Complete each of these *"I Love Lucy"* episode titles.

1 "Off _____
_____"

2 "The Ricardos Dedicate a
_____"

3 "The _____ Complex"

4 "Lucy Thinks Ricky Is
_____ ____
_____ ___"

5 "Deep _____ _____"

6 "The _____ Trip"

7 "_____ ___ _____ Scotland"

8 "L.A. _____ _____!"

9 "_____ and _____"

10 "_____ Are _____"

11 "_____ _____ Tulips"

12 "Building a _____"

13 "Lucy Is Jealous of _____
_____"

14 "Lucy _____ the _____"

15 "_____ _____ Biz
_____ _____"

16 "_____
_____Booking"

17 "Too _____ _____"

18 "The _____ Upstairs"

19 "The _____ Train _____"

20 "Young _____"

21 "_____ Hawaiian
_____"

22 "Never ___ _____ with
_____"

23 "The _____ _____ Story"

24 "Cuban _____"

25 "Changing the _____ _____"

26 "_____ Night in _____"

27 "The _____ Change
_____"

28 "_____ Island _____"

29 "No _____ Allowed"

30 "_____ _____ Hangs
___"

95 The Ending Credits

"I Love Lucy" debuted October 15, 1951 and ran on prime-time television for six seasons. During their run, the cast and crew created some of the most memorable moments in television history. Match each crew member with his or her job title(s).

1. Jack Aldworth
2. Desi Arnaz
3. William Asher
4. Ralph Berger
5. Herb Browar
6. Dann Cahn
7. Bob Carroll, Jr.
8. Kerwin Coughlin
9. Larry Cuneo
10. Eliot Daniel
11. Marc Daniels
12. Max Factor
13. Karl Freund
14. Robert de Grasse
15. Wilbur Hatch
16. Dick Henrikson
17. Sid Hickox
18. Ed Hillie
19. Elois Jenssen
20. James V. Kern

21. Irma Kusely
22. Hal King
23. Cam McCulloch
24. Bud Molin
25. Argyle Nelson
26. E.C. Norton
27. Ted Offenbecker
28. Jess Oppenheimer
29. James Paisley
30. Madelyn Pugh
31. Robert Reeve
32. Jay Sandrich
33. Bob Schiller
34. Lee Scott
35. Al Simon
36. Edward Stevenson
37. Maury Thompson
38. Jerry Thorpe
39. Bob Weiskopf

A Art Director

B Assistant Director

C Associate Producer

D Camera Coordinator

E Casting

F Choreographer

G Director

H Director of Photography

I Editorial Supervisor

J Executive Producer

K Film Editor

L Hair

M Makeup

N Music Director

O Music Editor

P Original Music

Q Producer

R Production Manager

S Property Master

T Rerecording Editor

U Set Dresser

V Sound Recorder

W Stage Manager

X Wardrobe

Y Writer

The *"I Love Lucy"* Episode Log

EPISODE NUMBER	EPISODE TITLE	ORIGINAL AIR DATE
1.	"Lucy Thinks Ricky Is Trying to Murder Her"	11/05/51
2.	"The Girls Want to Go to a Nightclub"	10/15/51
3.	"Be a Pal"	10/22/51
4.	"The Diet"	10/29/51
5.	"The Quiz Show"	11/12/51
6.	"The Audition"	11/19/51
7.	"The Seance"	11/26/51
8.	"Men Are Messy"	12/03/51
9.	"Drafted"	12/24/51
10.	"The Fur Coat"	12/10/51
11.	"Lucy Is Jealous of Girl Singer"	12/17/51
12.	"The Adagio"	12/31/51
13.	"The Benefit"	01/07/52
14.	"The Amateur Hour"	01/14/52
15.	"Lucy Plays Cupid"	01/21/52
16.	"Lucy Fakes Illness"	01/28/52
17.	"Lucy Writes a Play"	02/04/52
18.	"Breaking the Lease"	02/11/52
19.	"The Ballet"	02/18/52
20.	"The Young Fans"	02/25/52
21.	"New Neighbors"	03/03/52
22.	"Fred and Ethel Fight"	03/10/52
23.	"The Moustache"	03/17/52
24.	"The Gossip"	03/24/52
25.	"Pioneer Women"	03/31/52
26.	"The Marriage License"	04/07/52

27.	"The Kleptomaniac"	04/14/52
28.	"Cuban Pals"	04/21/52
29.	"The Freezer"	04/28/52
30.	"Lucy Does a TV Commercial"	05/05/52
31.	"The Publicity Agent"	05/12/52
32.	"Lucy Gets Ricky on the Radio"	05/19/52
33.	"Lucy's Schedule"	05/26/52
34.	"Ricky Thinks He's Getting Bald"	06/02/52
35.	"Ricky Asks for a Raise"	06/09/52
36.	"The Anniversary Present"	09/29/52
37.	"The Handcuffs"	10/06/52
38.	"The Operetta"	10/13/52
39.	"Job Switching"	09/15/52
40.	"The Saxophone"	09/22/52
41.	"Vacation from Marriage"	10/27/52
42.	"The Courtroom"	11/10/52
43.	"Redecorating"	11/24/52
44.	"Ricky Loses His Voice"	12/01/52
45.	"Sales Resistance"	01/26/53
46.	"The Inferiority Complex"	02/02/53
47.	"The Club Election"	02/16/53
48.	"The Black Eye"	03/09/53
49.	"Lucy Changes Her Mind"	03/30/53
50.	"Lucy Is Enceinte"	12/08/52
51.	"Pregnant Women Are Unpredictable"	12/15/52
52.	"Lucy's Show Biz Swan Song"	12/22/52
53.	"Lucy Hires an English Tutor"	12/29/52
54.	"Ricky Has Labor Pains"	01/05/53
55.	"Lucy Becomes a Sculptress"	01/12/53
56.	"Lucy Goes to the Hospital"	01/19/53
57.	"No Children Allowed"	04/20/53

58.	"Lucy Hires a Maid"	04/27/53
59.	"The Indian Show"	05/04/53
60.	"Lucy's Last Birthday"	05/11/53
61.	"The Ricardos Change Apartments"	05/18/53
62.	"Lucy Is Matchmaker"	05/25/53
63.	"Lucy Wants New Furniture"	06/01/53
64.	"The Camping Trip"	06/08/53
65.	"Ricky's Life Story"	10/05/53
66.	"Ricky and Fred Are TV Fans"	06/22/53
67.	"Never Do Business with Friends"	06/29/53
68.	"The Girls Go into Business"	10/12/53
69.	"Lucy and Ethel Buy the Same Dress"	10/19/53
70.	"Equal Rights"	10/26/53
71.	"Baby Pictures"	11/02/53
72.	"Lucy Tells the Truth"	11/09/53
73.	"The French Revue"	11/16/53
74.	"Redecorating the Mertzes' Apartment"	11/23/53
75.	"Too Many Crooks"	11/30/53
76.	"Changing the Boys' Wardrobe"	12/07/53
77.	"Lucy Has Her Eyes Examined"	12/14/53
78.	"Ricky's Old Girlfriend"	12/21/53
79.	"The Million-Dollar Idea"	01/11/54
80.	"Ricky Minds the Baby"	01/18/54
81.	"The Charm School"	01/25/54
82.	"Sentimental Anniversary"	02/01/54
83.	"Fan Magazine Interview"	02/08/54
84.	"Oil Wells"	02/15/54
85.	"Ricky Loses His Temper"	02/22/54
86.	"Home Movies"	03/01/54
87.	"Bonus Bucks"	03/08/54
88.	"Ricky's Hawaiian Vacation"	03/22/54

89.	"Lucy Is Envious"	03/29/54
90.	"Lucy Writes a Novel"	04/05/54
91.	"The Club Dance"	04/12/54
92.	"The Diner"	04/26/54
93.	"The Black Wig"	04/19/54
94.	"Tennessee Ernie Visits"	05/03/54
95.	"Tennessee Ernie Hangs On"	05/10/54
96.	"The Golf Game"	05/17/54
97.	"The Sublease"	05/24/54
98.	"Lucy Cries Wolf"	10/18/54
99.	"The Matchmaker"	10/25/54
100.	"The Business Manager"	10/04/54
101.	"Mr. and Mrs. TV Show"	04/11/55
102.	"Mertz and Kurtz"	10/11/54
103.	"Ricky's Movie Offer"	11/08/54
104.	"Ricky's Screen Test"	11/15/54
105.	"Lucy's Mother-in-Law"	11/22/54
106.	"Ethel's Birthday"	11/29/54
107.	"Ricky's Contract"	12/06/54
108.	"Getting Ready"	12/13/54
109.	"Lucy Learns to Drive"	01/03/55
110.	"California, Here We Come!"	01/10/55
111.	"First Stop"	01/17/55
112.	"Tennessee Bound"	01/24/55
113.	"Ethel's Hometown"	01/31/55
114.	"L.A. at Last"	02/07/55
115.	"Don Juan and the Starlets"	02/14/55
116.	"Lucy Gets in Pictures"	02/21/55
117.	"The Fashion Show"	02/28/55
118.	"The Hedda Hopper Story"	03/14/55
119.	"Don Juan Is Shelved"	03/21/55

120.	"Bull Fight Dance"	03/28/55
121.	"Hollywood Anniversary"	04/04/55
122.	"The Star Upstairs"	04/18/55
123.	"In Palm Springs"	04/25/55
124.	"Harpo Marx"	05/09/55
125.	"Dancing Star"	05/02/55
126.	"Ricky Needs an Agent"	05/16/55
127.	"The Tour"	05/30/55
128.	"Lucy Visits Grauman's"	10/09/55
129.	"Lucy and John Wayne"	10/10/55
130.	"Lucy and the Dummy"	10/17/55
131.	"Ricky Sells the Car"	10/24/55
132.	"The Great Train Robbery"	10/31/55
133.	"Homecoming"	11/07/55
134.	"The Recardos Are Interviewed"	11/14/55
135.	"Lucy Goes to a Rodeo"	11/28/55
136.	"Nursery School"	12/05/55
137.	"Ricky's European Booking"	12/12/55
138.	"The Passports"	12/19/55
139.	"Staten Island Ferry"	01/02/56
140.	"Bon Voyage"	01/16/56
141.	"Second Honeymoon"	01/23/56
142.	"Lucy Meets the Queen"	01/30/56
143.	"The Fox Hunt"	02/06/56
144.	"Lucy Goes to Scotland"	02/20/56
145.	"Paris at Last"	02/27/56
146.	"Lucy Meets Charles Boyer"	03/05/56
147.	"Lucy Gets a Paris Gown"	03/19/56
148.	"Lucy in the Swiss Alps"	03/26/56
149.	"Lucy Gets Homesick in Italy"	04/09/56
150.	"Lucy's Italian Movie"	04/16/56

151.	"Lucy's Bicycle Trip"	04/23/56
152.	"Lucy Goes to Monte Carlo"	05/07/56
153.	"Return Home from Europe"	05/14/56
154.	"Lucy and Bob Hope"	10/01/56
155.	"Lucy Meets Orson Welles"	10/15/56
156.	"Little Ricky Gets Stage Fright"	10/22/56
157.	"Little Ricky Learns to Play the Drums"	10/08/56
158.	"Visitor from Italy"	10/29/56
159.	"Off to Florida"	11/12/56
160.	"Deep Sea Fishing"	11/19/56
161.	"Desert Island"	11/26/56
162.	"Ricardos Visit Cuba"	12/03/56
163.	"Little Ricky's School Pageant"	12/17/56
164.	"Lucy and the Loving Cup"	01/07/57
165.	"Little Ricky Gets a Dog"	01/21/57
166.	"Lucy and Superman"	01/14/57
167.	"Lucy Wants to Move to the Country"	01/28/57
168.	"Lucy Hates to Leave"	02/04/57
169.	"Lucy Misses the Mertzes"	02/11/57
170.	"Lucy Gets Chummy with the Neighbors"	02/18/57
171.	"Lucy Raises Chickens"	03/04/57
172.	"Lucy Does the Tango"	03/11/57
173.	"Ragtime Band"	03/18/57
174.	"Lucy's Night in Town"	03/25/57
175.	"Housewarming"	04/01/57
176.	"Building a Barbecue"	04/08/57
177.	"Country Club Dance"	04/22/57
178.	"Lucy Raises Tulips"	04/29/57
179.	"The Ricardos Dedicate a Statue"	05/06/57
180.	"The *I Love Lucy* Christmas Show"	12/24/56
181.	Pilot	4/30/90*

*The *"I Love Lucy"* pilot served as the show's screen test and was not televised during the series' original run. Lost for years, the pilot was rediscovered and broadcast as a CBS special in 1990, *"I Love Lucy"*: The Very First Show."

Answers

1 First Things First
1. A (114)
2. "Lucy and Bob Hope"
3. false; Elizabeth Patterson, who also played Mrs. Trumbull, portrayed Mrs. Willoughby in "The Marriage License"
4. D (50)
5. B
6. Little Ricky laughs
7. "First Stop"
8. C
9. introduce Ricky to her "first" husband (5)
10. "Tennessee Ernie Visits" (94)

2 Seein' Stars
A. George Reeves (166)
B. Carmen Miranda (3)
C. Marilyn Monroe (103)
D. Harpo Marx (124)
E. Tallulah Bankhead (16)

3 All About Lucy
1. 1921 (138)
2. Esmeralda (22)
3. Dorrance and Company (90)
4. Bird Legs (105)
5. throw all the bills in the air; the bills that land face up are the ones that get paid
6. 12 (117)
7. "mousy brown" (72)
8. waffles (51)
9. *A Tree Grows in Havana* (17)
10. boo (112)
11. she reads a newspaper article about a housewife who made a fortune as a writer
12. Roberta
13. George Watson
14. August 6 (105)
15. 129 lbs.
16. Mrs. Hansen (68)
17. Hiawatha (59)
18. to sell Aunt Martha's old-fashioned salad dressing (79)

19. The Wednesday Afternoon Fine Arts League (47)
20. McGillicuddy

4 AKA Lucy
A. Miss McGillicuddy (35)
B. Pete (54)
C. Camille, Queen of the Gypsies (38)
D. The Maharincess of Franistan (31)
E. Sally Sweet (4)
F. Lucille McGillicuddy (79)
G. Isabella Klump (79)
H. Princess Lou-Cee (155)
I. The Professor (6)

5 Remembering Ricky
1. maracas (94)
2. Bicardi (26)
3. Carlos and Maria Ortega (28)
4. Nancy (40)
5. Ginny Jones (2)
6. *Don Juan*
7. "Lucy Goes to the Hospital"
8. Ricardo Alberto Fernando Ricardo de Acha
9. the Queen of England (142)
10. the Palladium (142)
11. Ricky plays the part of a hollow tree
12. Havana
13. Nick Bascopoulis (7)
14. Pedro, Pablo, Chu Chu, Josinte, and Jose (3)
15. a silver cigarette case (75)
16. Club Babalu
17. Prince Lancelot (38)
18. on Broadway (23)
19. Jimmy Demaret (96)
20. Marco
21. roast pig (133)
22. 5 feet, 11½ inches (134)
23. "no" (73)
24. Bennett Green

6 Occupational Hazard
Across
3. Buffo (6)
4. babysitter
6. psychiatrist (27)

8. Jerry
12. Abbott (55)
15. knife thrower (72)
18. crook (75)
19. Zeb (76)
20. Sherman (114)
21. Harris (83)
22. negligee (62)
23. waiter (73)
24. Handy Dandy (45)

Down
1. locksmith (37)
2. Beecher (97)
5. Bobby (114)
7. HEK (138)
9. Peterson (138)
10. Maurice (35)
11. business (100)
13. mindreader (105)
14. sheriff (112)
16. Wickes (19)
17. grocer (15)
21. Harvey (55)

7 Friends and Neighbors I
A. Sam Johnson (84)
B. Grace Foster (36)
C. Carolyn Appleby (125)
D. Mario Orsatti (158)
E. Mrs. Willoughby (26)
F. Arthur Morton (20)
G. Doug (93)
H. Mrs. Grundy (159)
I. Carlota Romero (from a scene in episode 78 that was cut from the final version)

8 Everything Ethel
1. C (121)
2. A (113)
3. A (113)
4. C (108)
5. D
6. A
7. A (7)
8. C (79)
9. B (29)
10. C
11. C (113)
12. A (134)
13. B (57)
14. A (73)

15. B
16. C (113)
17. A
18. C (139)
19. C (92)

9 Going Places
1. Italy
2. Tennessee
3. California
4. Palm Springs
5. Hollywood
6. Scotland
7. Monte Carlo
8. Swiss Alps
9. Hawaiian
10. Florida
11. Staten Island
12. Paris or L.A.
13. Europe
14. Cuba

10 Brown Derby Dining
1. Lucy   D
   Ethel   D
   Fred   E
   William Holden   A
2. Gregory Peck, Walter Pidgeon, Ava Gardner
3. Gus
4. B
5. manicure scissors
6. true
7. Jimmy Durante

11 Hollywood Souvenirs
1. menus from The Brown Derby
2. old tin can run over by Cary Grant's left rear wheel
3. grapefruit autographed by Richard Widmark
4. orange autographed by Robert Taylor
5. chopsticks from Don the Beachcomber
6. ashtray from The Beverly Hilton

12 The Candy Factory
1. She never had enough money at one time to open a checking account.
2. The Acme Employment Agency
3. "People We Place Stay Put"
4. stenographer, bookkeeper, comptometer operator, dental technician, insurance adjustor, and PBX operator
5. Kramer's Kandy Kitchen
6. Lucy swats a fly
7. because she kept pinching the chocolates to see what kind they were
8. two
9. ironing and cooking
10. scouring powder
11. a seven-layer devil's food cake
12. Lucy and Ethel each get a five-pound box of chocolates
13. the wrapping department
14. he orders in breakfast from the local drugstore and pretends to make it himself
15. "Well, I had it thrown at me on one of the darkest days of my life."
16. A. Snodgrass
17. four pounds
18. "Dear teller, be a lamb and don't put this through 'til next month."
19. C
20. the drugstore called to tell Ricky that he left his hat behind

13 That's English?
1. deep sea
2. "spill the beans" and "let the cat out of the bag" (136)
3. McGillicuddy
4. extravagances
5. psychiatrist
6. "crying wolf" (98)
7. gossiping (24)
8. ulterior motive (49)
9. "stew in her own juices" and "her goose is cooked" (49)
10. "off her trolley" (49)
11. jealous
12. experience
13. "the die is cast" (22)
14. don't
15. "you have made your bed, now lie in it" (86)

14 My Favorite Redhead
All twenty-five episodes were loosely based on "My Favorite Husband."

15 Just The Facts
1. C
2. C
3. Thursday or Friday
4. true
5. Bob Carroll, Jr. and Madelyn Pugh
6. B
7. C
8. Jess Oppenheimer, Bob Carroll, Jr., and Madelyn Pugh
9. B
10. October 15, 1951

16 Food for Thought
Across
2. grocer (15)
3. bread (25)
6. catsup (145)
7. vega (30)
9. grapefruit
11. sardines (54)
14. snails (145)
17. Bent Fork
18. watercress

Down
1. beef or meat (29)
2. Grapes (150)
4. eggs (172)
5. spaghetti (114)
6. cheese (153)
8. ham (69)
10. toast
12. Sally (111)
13. orange
15. ALBOC (92)
16. T-bone (29)

17 The Christmas Quiz
1. "Santa brings the North Pole with him and slides down like a fireman."
2. five dollars
3. because he overprunes the first tree
4. "a half a buck"
5. mistletoe
6. ornament
7. true
8. the kitchen
9. three
10. B
11. a new set of drums and a bicycle
12. a Lionel train set
13. "Jingle Bells"

14. every year they go through the string of lights to find the bulb that is burned out
15. C

18 The Anniversary Quiz
1. a television set (42)
2. B
3. Grace works at a jewelry store and is able to save Ricky 20 percent on a string of pearls for Lucy's anniversary gift (36)
4. at the fights (2)
5. she serves rice for breakfast, circles their anniversary date on the calendar, and leaves her wedding ring lying around
6. six
7. B (82)
8. false (121)
9. C (121)
10. false (2)
11. Joseff Jewelry Company (36)
12. golf clubs (82)

19 The Vitameatavegamin Speech
friends
girl
tired
run-down
listless
parties
unpopular
problems
little
bottle
vitamins
meat
vegetables
minerals
spoon
health
tablespoonful
so
tasty
candy
thousands
peppy
people
tomorrow

20 All About Little Ricky
1. A (80)
2. Stevie Appleby, by four days (71)

3. Superman (166)
4. true
5. B (163)
6. Mr. Crawford (156)
7. Ricky Ricardo, Jr. and his Dixieland Band (156)
8. "Five Foot Two, Eyes of Blue"
9. Stevie (166)
10. Bruce Ramsey (172)
11. "The Indian Show" (59)
12. Casino Parisien (162)
13. B (165)
14. Mrs. Trumbull
15. three (136)
16. tonsilitis (136)
17. Dr. Gettleman (136)
18. Room 602
19. Little Ricky and Fred are in the Ricardo living room. Fred is helping Little Ricky perfect his baseball swing. (154)
20. Billy Brown (163)
21. stage fright
22. doctor; drummer (157)
23. B (51)
24. Sherman's Music Company (157)
25. true (166)
26. Florence, Italy (149)
27. 11:00 a.m. (166)
28. nine (166)
29. Dr. Joe Harris (56)

21 Fowl Play
1. B (72)
2. in a barn in rural Italy (151)
3. *Millikan's Chicken-Mash Hour* (95)
4. 500
5. *Chicken Breeders' Gazette* (171)
6. "Off to Florida"
7. five dozen
8. inside Ethel's hat box (172)
9. Ernie Ford and His Four Hot Chicken Pickers (95)
10. "Lucy Raises Chickens"
11. inside Ethel's camera bag (147)
12. Little Ricky and Bruce Ramsey (172)
13. "lay that egg" (72)

14. "cheap, cheap, cheap" (171)
15. "Job Switching" (39)
16. "I've been henpecked" (171)
17. "You're a cute little chicken." (34)
18. "Be A Pal"
    "Men Are Messy"
    "Lucy's Bicycle Trip"
    "Lucy Raises Chickens"
    "Lucy Does the Tango"

22 Funny Foursome
Ethel
1. a fairy princess (163)
2. Albuquerque Elementary (175)
3. Yvette is a make-believe aunt Lucy invented to help explain the money in Ethel's suitcase in "Lucy Goes to Monte Carlo." (152)
4. Oscar (29)
5. nineteen (148)

Lucy
1. saxophone (40)
2. a big, fat pig
3. Zeb Allen of Allen's Used Clothing Emporium (76)
4. She's expecting Ricky to bring home a Hollywood talent scout who is looking for a Marilyn Monroe type.
5. "The Diet" (4)

Fred
1. "The Claw and Cackle Club" (69)
2. He's been charging the Ricardos ten dollars more a month than any other tenant in the building.
3. Little Orphan Annie (63)
4. Steubenville
5. "Ricky and Fred Are TV Fans"

Ricky
1. Fernando (120)
2. New Orleans, the Rocky Mountains (110)
3. "The Brains" (167)
4. "Rancho Grande" (134)
5. Ralph Berger (131)

23 Episode ID
1. S
2. B
3. A
4. J
5. W
6. G
7. O
8. P
9. F
10. E
11. K
12. T
13. C
14. V
15. H
16. R
17. N
18. X
19. U
20. M
21. Y
22. L
23. D
24. Q
25. I

24 The Menagerie
1. French poodle
2. Mr. Ritter (15)
3. Pepito the Clown (52)
4. A. Swan
   B. Wolf
   C. Bull
   D. Fox
   E. Fishing
   F. Dog
   G. Chickens
5. snails (145)
6. true
7. tiger
8. dragon (144)
9. trained seal (33)
10. Sylvia Collins (62)

25 Friends and Neighbors II
A. Mrs. Porter (58)
B. Mrs. McGillicuddy (110)
C. Mr. Stanley (56)
D. Freddy Fillmore (32)
E. Mrs. Benson (61)
F. Mr. Ritter (15)
G. Jean Valjean Raymand (12)
H. Madame Lemond (19)
I. burlesque comic (19)

26 Sales Pitches
1. Vitameatavegamin (30)
2. Speedy Laundry (87)
3. A Big Hunk of America (92)
4. Aunt Sally's Pecan Pralines (111)
5. Phipps Department Store (101)
6. Squire Quinn's Tavern (38)
7. Aunt Martha's Old Fashioned Salad Dressing (79)
8. Pontiac (109)
9. Nelson Photofinishing Company (79)
10. Cement (23)
11. beef (29)
12. The Brown Derby (114)
13. The Starlight Roof (2)
14. Eperway (67)
15. A Little Bit of Cuba (92)
16. Mertz & Kurtz (19)
17. Schwab's Drug Store (116)
18. Handy Dandy Kitchen Helper (45)
19. Golden Drumstick Restaurant (111)
20. furniture (170)
21. Acme Employment Agency (39)
22. Corona Grandos (162)
23. MGM
24. Korwin's Hatchery (172)
25. Johnson's Meat Company (29)

27 Theme Song Sing-Along
1. she
   loves
   me
   happy
   quarrel
   love
   up
   kisses
   no
   one
   can
   my
   missus
   man
   heaven
   love
   Lucy
   I
   love
   Lucy
   loves
   me
2. "Lucy's Last Birthday"
3. B (60)
4. Harold Adamson
5. Columbia

28 In the Fifties
1. H (166)
2. E (79)
3. C (38)
4. G (148)
5. C (34)
6. F (121)
7. E (106)
8. D (56)
9. F (132)
10. E (102)
11. F (138)
12. E (97)
13. E (103)
14. G (159)
15. B (7)
16. E (102)
17. C (32)
18. G (144)
19. D (61)
20. C (18)
21. F (123)
22. F (132)
23. H (166)
24. E (84)
25. H (176)
26. G (157)
27. C (39)
28. F (126)
29. H (171)
30. C (36)
31. D (77)
32. B (7)
33. D (66)
34. C (44)
35. D (63)
36. E (92)
37. H (167)
38. G (150)
39. E (97)
40. E (108)
41. G (146)
42. E (84)
43. F (137)
44. G (150)
45. G (163)
46. G (161)
47. C (29)
48. D (72)

49. D (58)
50. H (179)

㉙ Members Only
1. The Wednesday Afternoon Fine Arts League (47)
2. The Motion Picture Mothers' Club
3. Club Babalu
4. The Society Matrons League (25)
5. true (137)
6. The Blue Bird Club (14)
7. her new cashmere sweater (47)
8. PTA (172)
9. C (13)
10. The Tropicana
11. The Mocambo (121)
12. "Friendship"
13. false, it is their eighteenth anniversary (2)
14. The Friends of the Friendless (60)

㉚ Incognito
A. "wicked city woman" (94)
B. player for the Cleveland Indians (154)
C. Ricky's agent, Lucille McGillicuddy (126)
D. woman from Mars (89)
E. a candy wrapper (39)
F. bicycle racer (151)
G. umpire (154)
H. painter (36)
I. Superman (166)

㉛ In the Running
1. Phoebe Emerson
2. Mr. Hickox
3. The Willoughbys (26)
4. Mr. Chambers (44)
5. Squire Quinn (38)
6. false; it's Mr.Snodgrass (39)
7. Carolyn Appleby; Charlie (69)
8. Mrs. Hammond (97)
9. Al runs a used-car lot in Brooklyn (108)
10. Ohio (111)
11. George Skinner (111)
12. William Abbott (55)
13. Mrs. Hansen (68)
14. Madame Lemond

15. Grayline Bus Tours (127)
16. to raise money to pay for their trips to Europe (137)
17. A (149)
18. Union Pacific (132)
19. Mayor Ferguson (144)
20. Yonkers

㉜ Remembering Marion
1. true
2. Norman (62)
3. B
4. Rhapahonic School For Girls (69)
5. Margie Liszt and Shirley Mitchell
6. C (72)
7. actress
8. B (72)
9. wooden shoes (153)
10. *Sabrina* (108)

㉝ Out of Place
1. Jane; all others are names of dogs in Ricky's nightclub act in episode 1.
2. Phoebe; all others are members of the Wednesday Afternoon Fine Arts League.
3. Nora; the others were girls' names Lucy was considering during her pregnancy. (51)
4. Strongs; the rest were guests at Lucy's surprise birthday party at the Tropicana. (60)
5. Mrs. Brinkman; the others are neighbors of the Ricardos in New York. (61, 165)
6. Hal; the rest played poker with Ricky in episode 3.
7. Marilyn Borden; the others each played more than one character on the show.
8. Chip Jackson; the rest are old vaudeville friends of Fred.
9. Mr. Stewart; the rest are bald men Lucy invites to the apartment in episode 34.
10. Pancho; the others are Ricky's brothers (3)

11. Don; all others are names of Lucy's old boyfriends. (78)
12. The Munsons; the rest were invited to Ricky and Fred's going-away party. (9)
13. Walter Pidgeon; the others are stars spotted by Lucy at The Brown Derby. (114)
14. Stephen; the rest are boys' names Lucy was considering during her pregnancy (51)
15. Hal Henderson; the others were Lucy's old boyfriends. (2)

㉞ My Baby and Me
1. Jimmy and Timmy Hudson (14)
2. C
3. "Ricky Has Labor Pains" (54)
4. Mrs. Trumbull
5. Dr. Joe Harris (56)
6. four months (153)
7. Ralph
8. Stevie Appleby (71)
9. A (2)
10. Charlie
11. twenty-five (15)
12. Babyface Ethel
13. "Baby Pictures," "Ricky Minds the Baby"
14. eleven (50)
15. a twenty-five-pound block of cheese (153)
16. Ricky gets involved in a football game on television.
17. racing little girls (64)
18. Little Barney (102)
19. Mr. Stanley (56)
20. Helen Erickson (138)
21. an impression of a baby crying (52)
22. false; Professor Bonanova gets the news (105)
23. Jane Sebastian (55)
24. "Rock-a-bye Baby" (50)
25. Fred Bigelow's (138)
26. 10 percent of the regular fare (153)
27. chickens (171)
28. Mary Jane Croft (153)
29. B (45)

35 Starstruck
1. Rock Hudson (123)
2. Van Johnson (114)
3. C (114)
4. D (114)
5. B (122)
6. Bob Hope (154)
7. Cornel Wilde (122)
8. any two of these names: Alan Ladd, Clark Gable, Ava Gardner, Bob Hope (127)
9. Shelley Winters; Judy Holiday (114)
10. Harpo Marx (124)
11. Charles Boyer (146)
12. Van Johnson (125)
13. Orson Welles (155)
14. at the Farmer's Market and at the pool (115, 127)
15. Rock Hudson (123)
16. C (123)
17. Lana Turner (116)
18. Claude Akins (161)
19. true (121)
20. George Reeves (Superman) (166)

36 Quotable Quotes
1. Fred (7)
2. Lucy as Lucille McGillicuddy (79)
3. Ethel (53)
4. Fred (89)
5. Lucy (159)
6. Cousin Ernie (94)
7. Ricky (32)
8. Nancy Johnson (84)
9. Zeke (112)
10. Lucy (2)
11. Uncle Alberto (162)
12. Mrs. Willoughby (26)
13. William Holden (114)
14. Fred (86)
15. Mrs. McGillicuddy (118)

37 On the Radio
1. A
2. *Mr. & Mrs. Quiz*
3. Eric
4.
   A. Theodore Roosevelt
   B. Wyoming
   C. November 19, 1863
5 true
6.
   A. "the collector of internal revenue"

B. "the sap runs every two years"
C. "to scrape the barnacles off her hull"
D. "Please let me sit down, this is making me sick."
7. five hundred dollars
8. Freddy Fillmore
9. *Females Are Fabulous*
10. Nancy

38 Facts on Fred
1. true (171)
2. true
3. false (119)
4. true (73)
5. true (40)
6. false; she lives in Indiana (105)
7. false (64)
8. true
9. true
10. true (113)
11. true (55)
12. false; he claims to be a real estate tycoon (102)
13. false
14. true (92)
15. false; Fred was a corporal (138)
16. false; he plays the part of a frog (163)
17. true (173)
18. true (139)
19. true (131)
20. true (139)

39 Friends and Neighbors III
A. Peggy Dawson (20)
B. George Skinner (111)
C. Ernie Ford (95)
D. Richard Widmark (127)
E. Mrs. Hansen (68)
F. Sam Carter (99)
G. Don Loper (117)
H. Evelyn Bigsby (153)
I. Teensy and Weensy (112)

40 With This Ring...
1. burning his little black book (2)
2. Ricky's last name is misspelled (26)
3. Sam Zabioni (2)
4. true (26)
5. A (3)
6. The Eagle Hotel (26)
7. 1940 (26)
8. B (82)
9. Bert Willoughby (26)
10. Marion Strong (115)

41 ...I Thee Wed
1. D
2. C
3. H
4. A (102)
5. J
6. B (7)
7. G (48)
8. E (84)
9. F (167)
10. I
11. M (81)
12. R
13. S (9)
14. K (29)
15. P
16. T (37)
17. L (28)
18. Q (83)
19. N (106)
20. O (134)

42 The Pet Department
1. Alice is a bird
   Fred is a puppy
   Hopalong is a frog
   Jimmy is a turtle
   Mildred is a goldfish
2. a lizard (165)
3. D (165)
4. B (165)
5. Mr. Stewart (165)
6. she eats dog biscuits (165)
7. "The Indian Show" and "Ricky's Contract"
8. Elmer
9. weasel (22)

43 Instant Recall
1. L
2. Q
3. S
4. C
5. M
6. A
7. T
8. Y
9. G
10. D
11. B
12. N

13. F
14. P
15. H
16. K
17. X
18. J
19. W
20. E

44 Your Name, Please?
Across
1. Butch (4)
6. Teensy or Weensy (112)
9. Grace
10. Phoebe
11. Ginny (2)
14. Tennessee Ernie
17. Will (113)
19. Fred
21. Lillian (47)
23. Camille (38)
24. Ralph

Down
1. Bobby
2. Tom (49)
3. Joe (67)
4. Percy (53)
5. Freddy (5)
7. Stevie
8. Maggie (8)
12. Arthur (20)
13. Diana (177)
15. Sally (4)
16. Matilda
18. Bill (77)
20. Ethel
22. Lucy

45 Harpo Marx
1. because Carolyn is
   expecting to visit Lucy
   and all of Lucy's movie
   star friends
2. Hawaii
3. C
4. Gary Cooper
5. Carolyn's glasses
6. true; although it isn't
   seen, Carolyn
   mentions it
7. next door to "borrow
   some sugar"
8. He's performing at a
   women's club benefit
   luncheon.
9. "Take Me Out to the
   Ball Game"
10. Clark Gable

11. B
12. 315
13. Chico and Groucho Marx
14. at the hotel pool
15. C

46 The Telephone Directory
1. I (164)
2. K (90)
3. A (149)
4. J (134)
5. B (114)
6. G (119,126)
7. D (56), E (62), M (134),
   N (170)
8. C (79)
9. F (21)
10. H (62, 66), L (108, 113,
    118, 149)
11. K (2)

47 The Puppy Puzzle
1. Butch (4)
2. Cap (127)
3. Cocker (142)
4. Beagle (26)
5. Fred (165)
6. Rocky (141)
7. Bulldog (23)
8. Poodle (142)
9. Theodore (1)
10. hound (94)
11. Pekinese (107)
12. Mr. Stewart (165)
13. Collie (142)
14. Tillie (7)
15. poodle (103)

48 Behind the Scenes
1. D
2. A
3. G
4. B
5. H
6. I
7. C
8. E
9. F

49 Friends and Neighbors IV
A. Ralph Ramsey (177)
B. Sir Clive Richardson (143)
C. Helen Erickson Kaiser
   (138)
D. Angela Randall (143)
E. Mayor Ferguson (144)
F. Arthur "King Cat" Walsh
   (77)

G. Professor Falconi (72)
H. Phoebe Emerson (81)
I. Nancy Graham (133)

50 Doctor's Orders
1. A. Little Ricky's
      pediatrician (136)
   B. Diagnoses Ricky with
      morning sickness (54)
   C. Diagnosed the
      "gobloots." (16)
   D. Says "nursery school
      does not take the place
      of a home." (136)
   E. Psychiatrist (27)
   F. Lucy's baby doctor
      (56)
   G. Author of "How To
      Keep the Honeymoon
      from Ending" (3)
   H. a.k.a. Chuck Stewart
      (46)
2. C (157)
3. She assumes a celebrity
   identity, develops
   amnesia, and reverts
   to childhood. (16)

51 Multiple Mertz
1. A
2. B (38)
3. A
4. B
5. A (105)
6. A (24)
7. B (76)
8. A
9. B (27)
10. C (23)
11. B (95)
12. B
13. D (116)
14. C
15. B (152)

52 Everything's Relative
1. J
2. I
3. E
4. L
5. K (67)
6. B
7. H (112)
8. F (162)
9. D (26)
10. S (177)
11. C (14)
12. O (162)
13. A (78)

14. T (94)
15. P (49)
16. M (102)
17. N (3)
18. G (29)
19. R (55)
20. Q (158)
21. X (94)
22. Y (143)
23. V (152)
24. U (153)
25. W (175)

53 Friends and Neighbors V
A. Will Potter (113)
B. "Rattlesnake" Jones (135)
C. Walter Reilly (126)
D. Ben Benjamin (103)
E. Miss Lewis (15)
F. Mrs. Hudson (14)
G. Harry Henderson (49)
H. Betty Ramsey (178)
I. Charlie Appleby (71)

54 Name That Tune
1. "Ricky's European Booking"
2. C (14)
3. "The Straw Hat Song"
4. B (104)
5. B (112)

55 Hide and Seek
1. chocolates (39)
2. She doesn't want him to know that she is working for Mario. (158)
3. eggs (172)
4. William Holden (114)

56 The Numbers Game
1. room 602 (136)
2. Lucy assumes that her mother and Little Ricky will be traveling in the compartment next to hers, but Lucy and Ricky have compartment A in car 108, while Mrs. McGillicuddy's ticket is for compartment B in train car 107.
3. First, because the apartment only has only one bedroom, the Bensons will no longer have a second (empty) bedroom to remind them

that their daughter is gone. Second, the rent for the new apartment is less than for their former apartment.
4. Tenants:
   1. D (36)
   2. A (61)
   3. C (36)
   4. B (42)
   5. C (84)
   6. E (97)
5. "The Million-Dollar Idea"
6. room 354 (56)
7. It's the bridal suite. (149)
8. A (61, 72)
9. true
10. room 925

57 Grape-Stomping Stumpers
1. "Lucy's Italian Movie"
2. Lucy
3. Rome
4. She wants to "soak up some local color."
5. pizza pies
6. Turo
7. *Bitter Grapes*
8. Vittorio Fellipi
9. after
10. suite 605
11. Rosa
12. C
13. 150
14. Teresa Tirelli

58 Friends and Neighbors VI
A. Dan Jenkins (43)
B. Andrew Hickox (100)
C. Mother Willoughby (26)
D. Alvin Littlefield (33)
E. Kenneth Hamilton (141)
F. Bobby the Bellboy (116)
G. Billy Hackett (113)
H. Tom Henderson (49)
I. Eddie Grant (62)

59 The Grauman's Chinese Theatre Quiz
1. "To my darlin'— another Marlon"
2. suite 317
3. The Beverly Hilton Hotel
4. it was run over by Cary Grant's left rear wheel
5. *The Tall Men*
6. approximately 1:30 a.m.
7. *Blood Alley*

8. Count
9.
   A. Swanson
   B. Lloyd
   C. Power
   D. Grable
   E. Crawford
   F. Cooper
   G. Wayne
10. B
11. Lucy agrees to let Ethel keep the footprints under her bed every other month.
12. true
13. B
14. true
15. in the Mertzes' hotel suite
16. three
17. she thinks they're the work of "Freddie the Forger"
18. Little Ricky
19. four

60 All About Lucy II
1. C (49)
2. A (122)
3. B (8)
4. D (120)
5. C
6. B (89)
7. A (52)
8. B (152)
9. B (50)
10. B (19)
11. A (121)
12. B (31)
13. B
14. B (132)
15. C (92)
16. B (71)
17. B (78)
18. B
19. A (69)
20. B (102)
21. D

61 Recollections of Ricky
1. B
2. C (105, 162)
3. B (20)
4. B (65)
5. A (104)
6. B (37)
7. A (95)
8. D (99)
9. B
10. D

11. D (8)
12. D (168)
13. C (97)
14. B (115)
15. B (94)
16. A (66)
17. C (104)
18. A (45)

62 The Haberdashery

Across
3   loving cup (164)
4   Jeri (85)
6   headdress
8   Brown
9   Derby (114)

Down
1   Boyer (146)
2   Mulford (85)
5   Cap (127)
6   Hedda (118)
7   Straw

63 Hooray for Hollywood
1.   Lucy and Ethel take a bus tour of the movie stars' homes and other Hollywood sights. (127)
2.   MGM
3.   The Brown Derby and Grauman's Chinese Theatre
4.   Share, Inc. (117)
5.   The Beverly Palms Hotel (125)
6.   Richard Widmark's (127)
7.   Frank Williams
8.   Onna (116)
9.   Don Loper (117)
10.   one hundred dollars (117)
11.   Alan Ladd (117)
12.   The Brown Derby (114)
13.   Dolores Donlon and Maggie Magennis (115)
14.   too many production problems (119)
15.   matador's costume (120)
16.   The Mocambo (121)
17.   The Farmer's Market (122)
18.   The Mirror Theatre (122)
19.   Charlie Pomerantz (118)
20.   Carolyn Appleby

64 Road Test
1.   Ohio (111)
2.   Bent Fork (112)
3.   Amarillo (113)

4.   Albuquerque (113)
5.   Hollywood
6.   Palm Springs (123)
7.   Beverly Hills (127)
8.   London (142)
9.   Scotland (144)
10.   Paris (146)
11.   Switzerland (148)
12.   Italy (149)
13.   Monte Carlo (152)
14.   Florida (159)
15.   Cuba
16.   Connecticut
17.   Miami (160)
18.   Turo (150)
19.   England (143)
20.   New Mexico

65 Who Am I?
1.   Harpo Marx (124)
2.   John Wayne (129)
3.   Arthur Morton (20)
4.   Tom O'Brien (21)
5.   Mrs. Hudson (14)
6.   Ted Kurtz (19)
7.   Zeb Allen (76)
8.   Mr. Watson (92)
9.   Martha (79)
10.   Ricky (163)
11.   Hans Conreid (43, 53)
12.   Kenneth Hamilton (141)
13.   Mr. Foster (31)
14.   Mr. Feldman (137)
15.   Carolyn Appleby
16.   Santa Claus (180)
17.   Orson Welles (155)
18.   Van Johnson (125)
19.   Mrs. Trumbull (171)
20.   Bob Hope (154)
21.   Irma (129)
22.   Billy Hackett (113)
23.   Mr. Taylor (168)
24.   Flo Pauline Lopus (94)
25.   Grace Foster (36)
26.   Mrs. Peterson (5)

66 First Name Basis
1.   Ethel
2.   Arthur (20)
3.   Pepito (52)
4.   Phoebe
5.   Bobby
6.   Butch (4)
7.   Ginny (2)
8.   Alberto (162)
9.   Lillian (47)
10.   Carolyn
11.   Betty

12.   Ruth (47)
13.   Ernie
14.   Peggy (20)
15.   Stevie
16.   Carlota (78)
17.   Grace
18.   Evelyn (153)
19.   Fred
20.   Vittorio (150)
21.   Cornel (122)
22.   Juan

67 Palm Springs Puzzler
1.   Matches:
      Lucy   E
      Ricky   C
      Fred   G
      Ethel   F
2.   Rock Hudson
3.   *Captain Lightfoot*
4.   to get away from the people who annoy them the most
5.   the Good Humor Man
6.   B
7.   Adele
8.   he whistled
9.   Dore Schary's secretary
10.   going to a baseball game
11.   A
12.   "Old Bossy"

68 Face the Music
1.   L
2.   J (14)
3.   F (59)
4.   H (26)
5.   N (125)
6.   K (154)
7.   I (4)
8.   A (69)
9.   O (102)
10.   C (112)
11.   E (95)
12.   M (52)
13.   G (50)
14.   B (138)
15.   D (113)

69 Friends and Neighbors VII
A.   Maurice (35)
B.   Barney Kurtz (102)
C.   Mr. Stewart (165)
D.   Mr. Beecher (97)
E.   Mr. Dorrance (90)
F.   Marion Strong (72)
G.   Teresa (150)
H.   Diana Jordan (177)
I.   Dominic Orsatti (158)

70 The Chicken or the Egg
1. C (31)
2. C (1)
3. A (123)
4. C (26)
5. A (154)
6. C (68)
7. A
8. D (64)
9. B (53)
10. A (124)
11. B (7)
12. C (28)
13. D (16)
14. D (33)
15. B (16)
16. C (34)
17. B (3)
18. D (1)
19. B (16)
20. B (97)

71 Superstition
1. Mr. Meriweather (7)
2. Gemini (7)
3. the ace of spades (1)
4. Raya the Medium and Madame Ethel Mertzola
5. Adelaide (7)
6. three years (7)
7. true (7)
8. you're going to receive money (7)
9. a female visitor will be stopping by (7)
10. Scorpio (7)
11. Number matches:
   A   3
   B   5
   C   1
   D   7

72 Star Search
A. Bob Hope (154)
B. Hedda Hopper (118)
C. Orson Welles (155)
D. Rock Hudson (123)
E. Tennessee Ernie Ford (94)
F. Richard Widmark (127)
G. Van Johnson (125)
H. Charles Boyer (146)
I. Claude Akins (161)

73 Brand Name Match Game
1. J (45)
2. C (29)
3. S (68)

4. N (152)
5. R (81)
6. U (160)
7. Q (171)
8. M (109)
9. P (158)
10. B (106)
11. A (30)
12. W (111)
13. X (79)
14. L (108)
15. G (67)
16. I (101)
17. Y (39)
18. H (85)
19. T (90)
20. Z (87)
21. E (93)
22. D (100)
23. V (104)
24. F (31)
25. K (111)
26. O (116)

74 Trick or Treat
1. William Abbott (55)
2. waffles
3. "Lucy Fakes Illness"
4. He unplugs the clock.
5. She buys wax tulips.
6. chocolate bar (149)
7. a twenty-five-pound block of cheese (153)
8. She tells them that Ricky will star in the play if she's allowed to write it.
9. Because it's Ladies Day. According to Little Ricky, "Ladies and little boys get in free."
10. She disguises herself as George Watson, the fourth barbershop singer.

75 The Common Link
1. Scotland; the others are places the Ricardos and Mertzes visited while in Europe
2. cat; the others were pets kept by Little Ricky
3. Gulf & Western; the others were sponsors of *I Love Lucy*
4. *Be a Pal*; the others are programs hosted by Freddy Fillmore

5. Arnone; the others are last names of *I Love Lucy* scriptwriters
6. Green; the others are names of doctors
7. Jean; the others are middle names of Ethel Mertz
8. "Lucy's Schedule"; the others are episodes in which Vivian Vance does not appear
9. baseball glove; the others are anniversary presents Lucy and Ricky give each other
10. "The Publicity Agent"; the others are Hollywood-based episodes

76 Undercover Ethel
A. the Maharincess' assistant (31)
B. Madame Mertzola, a.k.a. Raya the Medium (7)
C. Mary Margaret McMertz (79)
D. Miriam Chumley (35)
E. Lily of the Valley (38)

77 Eating Habits
1. chocolates (39)
2. a sandwich
3. salad dressing (79)
4. vitamins, meat, vegetables, and minerals (30)
5. Crepe Suzette (12)
6. pizza dough
7. "Shortn'in' Bread" (113)
8. false; the sandwich had no jelly (58)
9. hot dogs (154)
10. perfume atomizer
11. a loaf of bread, wax paper, mayonnaise, and flour
12. hash
13. strawberry shortcake and gooseberry pie
14. pistachio ice cream with hot fudge and sardines

78 Perfectly Puzzling
1. Pepito (52)
2. pockets (27)
3. Preem (77)
4. Elizabeth Patterson
5. Percy (53)
6. poop out at parties (30)
7. Hippity-Hoppity (163)

8. Tropicana
9. Phipps (101)
10. Prince Lancelot (38)
11. Palm Springs (123)
12. "Pass That Peace Pipe"
13. Harpo (124)
14. Phoebe (81)
15. *The Pleasant Peasant* (38)
16. Pickpocket Pearl (66)
17. patio (176)
18. The Perils of Pamela (17)
19. The Professor (6)
20. *The Most Happy Fella* (174)
21. Pontiac (109)
22. Peggy (20)
23. pearls (36)
24. Pomerantz (25)

79 To Tell the Truth
1. one hundred dollars
2. true
3. 1. C
   2. B
   3. E
   4. A
   5. D
4. She sings like a chicken.
5. Carolyn's
6. Professor Falconi

80 Lucy Goes to Scotland
1. true
2. Lucy's great, great, great grandfather
3. Enchilada Ricardo
4. Mayor Ferguson
5. C
6. she can't do the "Sword Dance"
7. Scotty MacTavish MacDoogal MacCardo
8. B
9. Scottish towns that border Kildoonan
10. Enchilada Ricardo

81 Musical Moments
1. F (45)
2. J (19)
3. P (138)
4. T (95)
5. H (137)
6. Q (86)
7. N (144)
8. S (26)
9. A (4)
10. C (50)
11. E (52)

12. R (125)
13. G (135)
14. K (60)
15. D (154)
16. M (18)
17. N (144)
18. B (112)
19. U (173)
20. L (13)
21. C (50)
22. L (13)
23. K (60)
24. I (65)
25. O (59)

82 Complete the Quote
1. "brownstone bosom" (21)
2. "heifer" (94)
3. "penniless bum" (126)
4. "trained seal" (33)
5. "beer"; "pretzel" (58)
6. "knee-deep"; "stagnation"(41)
7. "staying on a subject" (57)
8. "like him" (95)
9. "'potamus" (106)

83 Take a Number
1. 155 (153)
2. B78455629G
3. 4,000 (160)
4. eight dollars
5. 19 (154)
6. two hundred
7. twenty-two (97)
8. thirty (167)
9. five (18)
10. twenty-two
11. thirteen (25)
12. three hundred dollars
13. 423 (116)
14. fifty-four (112)
15. 23 percent (30)
16. seventy-five
17. seven hundred
18. Pier 5 (160)
19. $3,272.65
20. 26 and 18

84 Friends and Neighbors VIII
A. Dr. Peterson (138)
B. Vittorio Fellipi (150)
C. Miss Hanna (155)
D. Frank Williams (116)
E. Jimmy Hudson (14)
F. Eleanor Harris (83)
G. Timmy Hudson (14)

H. Percy Livermore (53)
I. Dorothy Cooke (99)

85 The Truth About Ethel
1. false; she is from New Mexico
2. true (69)
3. true (113)
4. true (9)
5. true
6. true (21)
7. false; it is forty cents per quart (79)
8. true (29, 134)
9. true (175)
10. true (139)
11. false; it is Potter (113)
12. true
13. true (1)
14. false; she was mistaken for Pickpocket Pearl (66)
15. false; she was Miss Albuquerque (113)
16. true (175)
17. true
18. true
19. true (137)
20. false; Ethel says this about Betty Ramsey (175)

86 The Fashion Show
1. Lucy overhears Don Loper and Sheila MacRae discussing it
2. five hundred dollars
3. Pomona
4. Jane Sebastian
5. size 12
6. tweed suit
7. "a couple of marshmallows"
8. Share, Inc.
9. C
10. Mrs. William Holden, Mrs. Richard Carlson, Mrs. Van Heflin, Mrs. Gordon MacRae, Mrs. Dean Martin, Mrs. Forrest Tucker

87 Critic's Choice
1. "Ricky's Movie Offer"
2. "The Great Train Robbery"
3. "The Kleptomaniac"
4. "Lucy's Last Birthday"
5. "Lucy Hires An English Tutor"
6. "The Young Fans"

7. "Drafted"
8. "Lucy Is Envious"
9. "The Black Eye"
10. "L.A. at Last"

88 Do You Know?
1. *Don Juan*
2. Kildoonan (144)
3. London (142)
4. Ricky Ricardo Fan Club (119)
5. Bulldog Cement (23)
6. dog
7. Gale Gordon
8. window ledge
9. Yankee Doodle Day (179)
10. Doctor Peterson (138)
11. Don Loper (117)
12. dollar (87)
13. Dorothea Wolbert (137)
14. voodoo (56)
15. Sam & Dorothy (99)
16. Lucy Ricardo
17. Dorrance and Company (90)
18. Theodore (1)
19. London Palladium (142)
20. Dore Schary (119)
21. dozing (86)
22. hot dog vendor (154)
23. Union Pacific Domeliner (131)
24. gondolier (158)
25. downstairs (42)

89 That Never Happened!
1. D
2. D
3. C
4. C
5. B
6. C
7. C
8. C
9. A
10. C

90 Lucy's Loving Cup
1. because Ricky laughs at the new hat Lucy brings home and tells her that she'd look better wearing the loving cup
2. Flatbush Avenue in Brooklyn
3. for being the "winningest jockey of all time"
4. $49.95

5. 4,961
6. Hazel
7. Lucy loses the veil at the Spring Street subway stop.
8. Bleecker Street
9. change out of her blue jeans
10. a fuzzy fish bowl

91 Lasting Impressions
1. Harcourt
2. Fred the dog
3. true
4. Ricky carries Lucy off the set (30)
5. a suit of armor
6. Pepito
7. Bob Carroll, Jr.
8. D

92 Lyrical Lucy
1. "There's a Brand New Baby at Our House" (45)
2. "Cuban Pete/ Sally Sweet" (4)
3. "Ricochet Romance" (112)
4. "We're Having a Baby" (50)
5. "Forever Darling" (137)
6. "California, Here I Come" (110)
7. "Man Smart, Woman Smarter" (173)
8. "We'll Build a Bungalow" (13)
9. "I'm in Love with a Dragon's Dinner" (144)
10. *"I Love Lucy"* theme song (60)

93 Final Thoughts
1. C (178)
2. A (90)
3. A (164)
4. B (163)
5. B (117)
6. B (166)
7. C
8. A (103)
9. A (89)
10. B (63)
11. A (144)
12. B (139)
13. A (177)
14. A (152)
15. B

16. B (160)
17. B
18. C (137)
19. A (125)

94 Finishing Touches
1. to Florida
2. Statue
3. Inferiority
4. Trying to Murder Her
5. Sea Fishing
6. Camping
7. Lucy Goes to
8. at Last
9. Mertz; Kurtz
10. Men; Messy
11. Lucy Raises
12. Barbecue
13. Girl Singer
14. Misses; Mertzes
15. Lucy's Show; Swan Song
16. Ricky's European
17. Many Crooks
18. Star
19. Great; Robbery
20. Fans
21. Ricky's; Vacation
22. Do Business; Friends
23. Hedda Hopper
24. Pals
25. Boys' Wardrobe
26. Lucy's; Town
27. Ricardos; Apartments
28. Staten; Ferry
29. Children
30. Tennessee Ernie; On

95 The Ending Credits
1. B
2. J
3. G
4. A
5. W
6. I, K
7. Y
8. E
9. A
10. P
11. G
12. M
13. H
14. H
15. N
16. S
17. H
18. B
19. X
20. G
21. L
22. M
23. U
24. K
25. R
26. O
27. V
28. Q, Y
29. B
30. Y
31. T
32. B
33. Y
34. F
35. C
36. X
37. D
38. B
39. Y

Photo Credits

CBS Worldwide, Inc.: p. 17

Desilu, Too: pp. 6, 7a, 7b, 7c, 7d, 8, 9a, 9b, 9c, 9d, 9e, 9f, 9g, 9i, 10, 11, 12a, 12b, 12c, 12d, 12e, 12f, 12g, 12h, 15, 16, 18, 19, 20, 23, 27, 29, 30, 32, 35a, 35b, 35c, 35d, 35e, 35f, 35g, 35h, 35i, 36, 37, 39, 41a, 41b, 41c, 41e, 41f, 41g, 41h, 41i, 43, 44, 45, 46, 47, 49, 50, 51, 52, 53a, 53b, 53c, 53d, 53e, 53f, 53g, 53h, 53i, 54, 55, 56, 61, 62, 63a, 63b, 63c, 63d, 63e, 63f, 63g, 63h, 63i, 64a, 64b, 64c, 64d, 64e, 64f, 64g, 64h, 64i, 65, 67, 69a, 69b, 69c, 69d, 69e, 69f, 69g, 69i, 71, 72a, 72b, 72c, 72d, 74, 75a, 75b, 75c, 75d, 75e, 75f, 75g, 75h, 75i, 77, 79, 81, 83, 84-85, 89, 90, 91a, 91b, 91c, 91d, 91e, 91f, 91g, 91h, 91i, 94, 95a, 95b, 95c, 95d, 95e, 95f, 95g, 95h, 95i, 98, 99, 100a, 100b, 100c, 100d, 100e, 101, 102-103, 104, 105, 106, 107, 109a, 109b, 109c, 109d, 109e, 109f, 109g, 109h, 109i, 111, 112, 113, 118, 119, 121, 123

The Lucy-Desi Museum: pp. 7e, 12i, 22, 41d, 87, 97, 116, 125

Courtesy Desi Arnaz, Jr.: p. 4

Ric Wyman Collection: pp. 9h, 13, 14, 21, 24, 25, 31, 33, 59, 60, 69h, 70, 82, 93, 115, 117